INSIDER'S GUIDE
TO THE ART
OF PERSUASION

Use Your Influence to Change Your World

Dr. Rick Kirschner
Ashland, Oregon, USA

ISBN 978-0-6151-5631-6

Talk Natural Press
A Division of The Art of Change LLC

The Art of Change books and multimedia programs are available at special quantity discounts to use as premiums and sales promotions, or for use in corporate training programs. For more information, please write to the Director of Special Sales, The Art of Change LLC, P.O. Box 896, Ashland, OR 97520. Or contact your local bookstore.

Dedicated to the change artists in our world, the dreamers and doers who care passionately about the future; Who recognize that change is inevitable, but progress is not; Who seek out opportunities to improve whatever is in front of them or given to them; Who work tirelessly, often with little recognition or acclaim, to bring about positive and worthwhile change; Who guarantee through their labors that even when today is good, tomorrow will be better than today.

Acknowledgements

Thanks to my many teachers, mentors and guides in the art of persuasion; to my ever-patient and cheerful wife, Lindea, who shared the vision and helped me bring it to fruition; to my daughter Aden, whose thoughtful insights and way with words has been a great help to me; to Hal Dresner, whose remarkable wit, stories and gift for language helped me take the important next step on the project; to Bucky Fuller, whose inspired teaching helped me understand that the best way to get people to make a change is to build the bridge to a better future; to my friends who supported me in finding new inspiration in this stage of my life, including Jon, Sally, Will and Jeff; and to Rollie, my faithful companion who let me ignore him when I needed to meet deadlines.

TABLE OF CONTENTS

TABLE OF CONTENTS (cont'd)

INTRODUCTION

People love to be right, even about being wrong. But in the Art of Persuasion, if you have to be right, you're doing it wrong. Persuasion finds success in meeting people where they are, first understanding and then speaking to their needs, interests and motivations.

There are two important reasons to learn the Art of Persuasion. First, you've got to know how to protect yourself from unscrupulous people with hidden agendas who use ignorance and emotion to bring about negative ends.

Second, consider how many great ideas have disappeared into the mists of time because of a failure to persuade. Think of the opportunities squandered, the resources wasted, and the money and income lost because the right person at the right time lacked the persuasive skill to persuade the key people to take the necessary actions. If you have the answer to a question, or the solution to a problem, and you are unable to persuade others, the people who need that answer or solution have no hope. Your business, your family, your community, your country and the world itself may one day depend on your persuasion skills.

That's where this book comes in. The ideas and insights I'm about to reveal to you have the potential to dramatically increase your influence on the world around you. No more will you be misled or deceived into making decisions that work against your interests. It is my hope that, as a result of what you learn here, you will create a more positive future for yourself, your family, and our world.

I do not claim to have all the answers. I recognize the value in your own experiences. So I invite you to consider this material as a personal learning laboratory, a safe place to discover what you know and what you don't know, what you use and don't use, what's being done to you, what you can do and what you must do in order to have the influence you deserve in creating a better tomorrow. And when all is said and done, I hope you enjoy this exploration into the amazing designs and practical patterns of the Art of Persuasion.

1

USEFUL DEFINITIONS

Influence

What is influence? Is influence something you have or something you do? Pardon the paradox, but the answer is both. When people trust you, they are open to being persuaded by you, and your influence flows into them as a force that is recognized and respected. This natural process gives you the power to cause things to happen through others with their willing consent. Trust is so important to positive persuasion that I've devoted an entire chapter to building it, and trust runs as a thread that connects all of the material in this book. Trust magnifies your persuasive power, and there is nothing so powerful as the positive influence trust makes possible.

Negative Influence

Yet there is also such a thing as negative influence. That's when you are persuaded or motivated to act against your own interests, or you persuade others to act against their interests. This kind of influence does not require trust. It does, however, require acceptance and acquiescence, through the surrendering of personal responsibility. It happens in a variety of ways. For example, peer pressure creates this kind of influence. Have you ever noticed how people take on at least some of the characteristics of the people with whom they spend the most time? Any time you go along with the crowd without considering the consequences, you run the risk of negative influence. When you try to gain some advantage by spending your time with people who don't care about you and want to use you for their own ends, you run the risk of negative influence.

Negative influence can also insert itself into your life when you limit the scope of your input. In this age of information, with radio stations, internet stations, TV stations, specialized magazines, newspapers and websites that promote a single point of view, people marginalize themselves and surrender important options as they watch, listen and read only that which supports their limited, and therefore limiting, views and opinions. In the dawning years of television and radio, advertisers, hosts and personalities admonished their audience with the classic "DON'T TOUCH THAT DIAL!"

When your mind is set on comfort and agreement without challenge, eventually you become enthralled to your chosen mental environment. The mind narrows, positions harden, society becomes polarized, and important information goes unnoticed because it exists outside the limited domain. If your intent is to gain leverage and natural influence, then narrowing your mind is foolish and dangerous.

I tell my students to TOUCH THE DIAL! Change the station; read, watch or listen to something that you disagree with, and challenge your views in order to gain access to information that exists outside of your comfort zone. In this way you can expand the scope of your input, and bring into your awareness other options, other interpretations and possibilities that provide you with what you need to better understand your world and give you sufficient information to influence it.

Coercion

Perhaps the most damaging kind of negative influence occurs when someone has power over you and requires your compliance. Whether that's a boss, a manager, a political leader or party, you have to do what they tell you to do. It's called coercion, and it comes with a price. The cost of coercion is the loss of trust.

Parents may fall into the coercion trap, when they force their children into compliance instead of using persuasion to build trust. "I'll give you something to cry about," shouts the mother in the supermarket line at her out-of-control baby. Children may be cowed by coercion, but then they become teens. The hormones hit their brains, they go temporarily insane, and their parents find themselves facing the serious repercussions of having no influence at all.

Employers and managers may intimidate their employees into apparent obedience, only to find themselves dealing with sabotage, subterfuge, backbiting and backstabbing. In business, from the boardroom to the assembly line, coercion is far too common. The boss stakes out a position, and her track record shows agreement is the desired response, and people who challenge the position aren't around for long. The manager or supervisor makes it clear that dialog isn't an option. "If you want to keep your job, you'll shut up and do what your told!"

Coercion restrains and inhibits. Coercion uses threats, isolation, deprivation and punishment as a means of control. Among its effects are phobias, anxiety attacks, and other behavioral disorders. Think this through and you'll realize just how nasty coercion can be. The threat of punishment, of disapproval, of provoking anger may gain compliance in the short term, but in the long term trust is lost and may be difficult, even impossible, to regain. Coercion almost always comes with a high cost. Coercive behavior rules out persuasion.

Persuasion

Persuasion facilitates. Persuasion connects point A to point B, by building a bridge between them. So what exactly is persuasion? For our purposes, it is a deliberate attempt to influence a person's attitude, using the means of communication. In order to make sense of this, let's break it down. Why deliberate? A deliberate attempt means it is not accidental or incidental, but done on purpose. Why influence a person's attitude? Attitude drives behavior!

Attitude = MAP

Attitude, for our purpose, is a person's MAP of reality regarding a particular subject or idea. That MAP consists of personal motivations, access language, and assumed positions.

Are people motivated to take positions on all kinds of things? Absolutely. Are you for the war or against the war? Are you pro-choice or pro-life? Do you think that the environment should be considered over special or private interests, or the reverse? Should the United Nations have more power or less power in the affairs of nations? Are you progressive, conservative, libertarian or green? Should employees do what they're told because employers see the big picture, or should employers listen to their employees because they have a better sense of what's actually going on? Are you pro-business or pro-labor? Whose interests matter most, the government or the individual? Are you in favor of the right to bear arms, or the right to bare arms? Do you prefer comedy, drama or action? Science fiction, historical fiction, or science and history without fiction? Which is better, chocolate or vanilla? Lunch out or lunch in? Which is better, healthy food or a healthy appetite? And why do you care about any of this at all?

When people are motivated to assume the position on something, when they decide they are for or against something, the meaningful shades of grey in between no longer get noticed. Reader take note: Those shades of grey constitute the domain where persuasion can occur.

The Art of Persuasion

Let's put this all together now. The art of persuasion is a skillful at-tempt to influence a person's attitude. A change in attitude (MAP) leads to a change in behavior. A change in behavior leads to a change in outcome.

There are many methods of persuasion. Some methods are ethical, and some unethical. Ethics is the domain of free will that lives between the rule of law and sheer anarchy. Ethics are, therefore, subjective. Just as you have your own sense of right and wrong, I have mine.

For example, I think it is unethical to intentionally use fear to influence voters. I think it is unethical to use the wilderness to sell cars and cigarettes, though the ad results are often amusing. I believe honesty is almost always the best policy because it gives you more sustainable long-term influence, though it may create short-term complications.

But those are my opinions. Ultimately, I leave it to you to

determine your own ethical sensibilities about where, when and how to use the art of persuasion. Meanwhile, there are professional persuaders all around you, seeking to direct your thoughts and actions by any means in order to achieve their negative ends. Yet you make the choices in your life, and the only thing that makes your compliance with their schemes possible is ignorance and emotion.

Manipulation

This brings me to the BIG question that ethical people must confront when learning to change the world with the art of persuasion. Is persuasion the same thing as manipulation? Again, please pardon my paradox, but the answer is YES, IT IS, and NO, IT IS NOT. Allow me to explain

Once upon a time, when you were an infant, you could not walk, and did not know how to speak in any comprehensible language. You used crying, staring and giggling to convey a host of different messages (I'm hungry, I'm sleepy, I'm wet, I'm frustrated, I have to burp, I'm a mess, I'm uncomfortable, I'm excited, I want to see you again, Where did you go? Don't go, etc.) You learned to walk and talk at a time in your life when NOBODY could tell you how to do it. You learned that if you wanted juice instead of milk or water, you had to say something specific. "Juice." And juice would come to you. You learned that you could get a particular person to bring it, if you had the right word. "Juice Mommy!" and "Juice Daddy!" Then you learned that you could accelerate the speed at which juice came to you, if you just had the right word. "Juice, Mommy, now!" And you learned that modulating your voice tone, and tempo, and volume, could make it come faster. "Juice, Mommy, NOWWWWWW!"

Why did you do this? What motivated you to master such complex skills? The answer is obvious. Your ability to enjoy your life depended on expanding the domain of your effectiveness beyond what your arms and voice could reach. You needed help. You still do.

Persuasive communication abilities are built right in to each of us, part of the amazing design of who you are. And you have used these skills your entire life. You may or may not have used them correctly. Now you have the opportunity to upgrade your knowledge of these skills, to use them more purposefully and effectively than at earlier stages of your life. And if you are concerned about manipulating others to act against their own interests, then don't!

If your concern is that others might use these same skills to manipulate you against your own interests, I have some important news for you. All it takes for you to be manipulated to act against your own interests is to surrender your ability to engage in critical thinking. That is the price of ignorance, and what you get when you trade reason for emotion. The failure to think for yourself endangers you, and the same holds true for everyone else as well. That is the last thing I would want in a reader. In fact, if you haven't already done so, I want you to put on your thinking cap now! I want you to fully engage your critical thinking skills, because thinking for yourself is essential to your understanding of the secrets contained in this book.

Just a few more definitions and we'll be ready to dig in and uncover the secrets for changing the world using the art of persuasion.

Persuader: That's you.

Persuadee: That is whomever you intend to persuade. A persuadee can be an individual, a small or large group.

Persuasion Proposition: This consists of the following. Who do you intend to persuade? What you want them to do,

think, and decide? Where do you intend to persuade them?
When do you intend to persuade them? How do you intend
to persuade (Openers, Themes, Guides, Cues.) Why do you
want to persuade, and why will your persuadee want you to
succeed?

Presentation: When it is your turn to present your persuasion proposition, we'll call that your presentation.

Three Phases of Persuasion: Listen, Transition, and
Presentation

Needs/Styles: Communication need expressed through
communication style

Openers: Transitional options for beginning your presentation

Guides: Ways to package your information to make it
more persuasive

Cues: Signals that speak to the emotions as indicators of
when to be persuaded

Close: Options for bringing persuasion efforts to a decision point

    And that completes our set of useful definitions. We
now have a shared frame of reference for exploring the useful assumptions through which persuasion becomes possible.

2

USEFUL ASSUMPTIONS

I'm going to assume that you communicate just fine
with most people. Even if that is not true, I'm going to assume that you are able to communicate just fine with at least
a few people.   However, if you can think of no one with
whom you are able to communicate just fine, that's fine.
Because you are about to dramatically improve your situation and station in life, increase your circle of influence and
expand your support system, by gaining the persuasive
power of useful assumptions.

To understand the relationship of your assumptions
to your results in communication and in life, I offer you a
model that I call 'The Nature of Sanity.'

For our purposes, sanity is that mental state in which
you think you know who you are, where you are, and in general, what's going on. To break it down a little further, first
you assume that you know something. Once you make an
assumption (about yourself, about others, about situations,

etc.) you inevitably will act as if your assumption is true. And your actions will have effects, in that you will find evidence in order to have the experience that your assumption is true. Said another way, you get to be right. Getting to be right is the booby prize in communication. (The booby prize is the prize given to the losers!) Let's say it yet another way. "For as you believe, so shall it be." Whatever you assume to be true, you act like it's true and look for proof. The nature of sanity is an exercise in self-fulfilling prophecy. While being right rarely leads to change, it frequently leads to conflict.

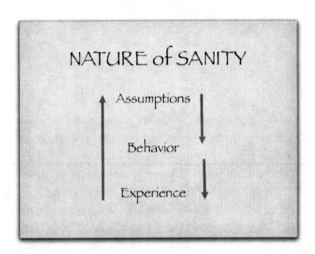

Fortunately for humanity, someone came up with the scientific method to overcome the blinders placed on us by the nature of sanity. The scientific method involves forming a working hypothesis (an assumption), then acting as if it isn't true (testing it, trying to disprove it) and if it remains standing after all that work, you think, hmmm, I guess I'm on to something! Thanks to the scientific method, the human race has experienced breakthrough after breakthrough in our understanding of the universe and our place in it. For most people, it isn't easy to have breakthroughs, because it seems to go against the nature of sanity.

The role of the nature of sanity in using the power of persuasion is fundamental. I'm not saying that you shouldn't make assumptions. You can't help it. And assumptions do play a key role in our ability to navigate in life. You wouldn't want to have to figure everything out all the time. The challenge with assumptions is to make useful ones rather than limiting ones. A useful assumption gives you enough informed perspective on your own behavior and the behavior of others that you can engage in behaviors that lead to worthwhile outcomes. A limiting assumption holds you back, ties you down, and traps you into self-defeating and counterproductive behavior.

So your assumptions can either facilitate your persuasive efforts or obstruct them. Your assumptions can enhance the tools offered in this book, or interfere with your ability to use them. Negative reactions, wrong interpretations, and polarizing positions constitute the interference and obstacles of interpersonal communication that occur as a result of limiting assumptions.

I conducted my training program,'The Art of Communication: How To Bring Out The Best In People...Even At Their Worst!" for a major automobile manufacturer. I had 45 plant managers together in a room. They all knew each other, and they had all shared stories with each other about the difficult people they had to manage. I was telling them about useful assumptions vs. limiting ones. I asked the group, "If you think someone is a jerk, how do you treat them?" And the group replied, "Like a jerk." I asked, "If you treat someone like a jerk, how does he act around you?" and the answer came back, "Like a jerk." Then I asked "And what do you say about him at that point?" And the group responded, "He's a jerk." Then I gave them a second example. I asked, "If you think someone is a moron, how do you talk to him?" And the answer came back "Like he's a moron!"

USEFUL ASSUMPTIONS

It was at this point that a rather large guy named Denny stood up in the back of the room, and told me in no uncertain terms that he had come to learn how to deal with a guy named Joe. "And believe me, Rick" he declared, "it's not an assumption on my part, it's a fact! Joe is a jerk and a moron!" I looked around the room, and noticed that everyone else was nodding their head in agreement. They all knew Joe. They all shared Denny's opinion of him. Maybe you know Joe and have the same opinion of him. Maybe you have people in your life that will nod their head in agreement whenever you describe certain people to them. I wouldn't be at all surprised. It turns out that it is pretty easy to find people to agree with anything that ties you up, holds you back, or traps you into self-defeating behavior. Why? Misery loves company.

It may be a bit more challenging to find people who will tell you this: Even if you can prove that someone is a jerk or moron in a court of law, that won't help you to get persuasive results. If you have to be right, you're doing it wrong. Your limiting assumptions about people limit your creativity and effectiveness, by triggering negative reactions in you, and cause you to engage in behaviors that lead to limiting and self-fulfilling outcomes. "I knew he wouldn't listen." "I knew she didn't care." Did you? Then you win the booby prize. You lose.

Now you may be thinking, "Yeah, but what if Joe really is a jerk and a moron?" Well, what if? Does it help you or hinder you to be right about that? Don't get me wrong. You are going to make assumptions. You have to assume something you will be able to do nothing at all. But useful assumptions em-power you, while limiting assumptions limit you. So if you must assume some-thing, assume something useful. You don't have to be right about a useful assumption. But you can use it to find a vector of approach, employ a method of persuasion, and create the possibility of success. This book is filled with useful rather than limiting assumptions. They may not always be true, but even if you try to disprove them, they will stand up to your test and prove their usefulness.

Here are a few useful assumptions to keep in mind:

You cannot not influence people

Yes, I know. That's a double negative, and as we've all been taught, two negatives make a positive. The point is that you constantly influence people with the things you say and don't say, do and don't do, and even what you think or don't think about them. In fact, the only way to have no influence with someone is if one of you is no longer alive! Assuming that both you and the person you seek to persuade are alive, you most assuredly have some influence.

Every time you ask a question or make a statement to someone, you are participating in his or her thought process. Every question, every statement, has a consequence, and in this way, you can and do shape the thoughts of others. You always have an impact! So put to rest any idea that you don't have influence. Instead, notice the influence that you do have, the responses that you do get. And if you don't like what you're getting, change what you're doing!

Questions have persuasive power

Have you ever been asked something and felt completely confused by it? Ever been asked a question and found yourself defending yourself against it's implication and inferences? A question takes the listener's mind down a particular road, whether it's the road of agreement or disagreement, of finding examples or finding counter-examples. It is entirely possible to ask a set of questions that changes a person's mind. It is entirely possible to ask a question that gets a conversation back on track, or takes it way off the beaten path. We set direction, expectation, and emotional reaction into motion with our questions. We create relevancy and expose motivation and intent with our questions.

Knowing you can do this, and knowing what you intend to do with this, gives you a lot of flexibility in terms of leading people where you want them to go. If influence is a given, then questions are a powerful intervention in the thinking of others. You can ask for relevance, intent, motivation, deeper understanding, and a whole host of other useful bits of information. Questions can provide possibilities to your persuadees, can invite thought, and solicit agreement. Most people have all the answers. It is the questions that they don't have. You can provide them.

Flexibility increases persuasive ability

I once had the opportunity to observe an aikido master. He was teaching children his martial art and he offered a demonstration to the parents in attendance. He asked the largest person in the room to step up and try to knock him down. There were some large parents there willing to give it a try. But no one could do it. In fact, no matter how hard they tried, they'd stumble and fall as they charged him, and then he'd catch them before they could fall. I was amazed. I blurted out "How are you doing that" And he turned, his eyes made contact with mine, and he said "Ah, grasshopper!" Then he explained that the essence of aikido is moving with, rather than away or against.

Sometimes, that means you must accept the unacceptable, in order to move with it and take charge over it. Only then can you redirect whatever is aimed at you towards your desired result.   Your stability is the center of your flexibility, and that stability comes from accepting what is. If you can't accept what is happening for what it is, you are already off balance, and contributing to your own downfall.

I think that is truly profound. After all, no matter what is happening in this moment of your life, whether you like it or don't like it, agree with it or don't agree with it, approve of it or don't approve of it, the truth is that it is what it is, it isn't what it isn't, and that's how it is. To be persuasive, you must learn to accept even the unacceptable, because your stability gives rise to flexibility, and flexibility increases your persuasive power.

Flexibility means having more than one choice, and getting feedback instead of failure. If you only know one way to do something, you'll always have to do it, even if it doesn't work! Consider the person whose only choice is to lose his temper when he doesn't get what he wants. He has no choice but to lose his temper, it's all he knows to do. A more flexible person could notice that losing his temper is creating more problems than it solves. A more flexible person could try whining instead! More than one choice means that if what you're doing isn't working, you can notice that and do something else. Feedback instead of failure means that you can learn from the consequences of your choices, and apply those learnings to do better next time around.

Resistance is a Result

Yes, some of the best ideas are met with resistance. Important solutions fail to be implemented because of resistance. For our purposes, if you meet resistance, it is useful to assume that you've put it there, to think of resistance as a form of feedback about how you've gone about your persuasive efforts.

There are, in fact, several ways to create sure-fire resistance in others. The first is insistence, the idea that persuasion is all about talking rather than listening, telling and selling instead of caring and sharing. When you find yourself insisting that someone understand something, or listen to you, or agree with your view, or you pour out information at them like a fire hose, there is a good chance that you are creating a negative reaction that will polarize your persuadees against what you have to say. Likewise, if you have resistance in yourself to the act of persuading others, your persuadees may feel your discomfort, take on your resistance and make it their own. If you're not persuaded, people tend to agree with you.

I recall an incident when I was a med student. One of my peers was recommending a dietary change to a patient. His problem was that he didn't like the item that he was recommending, and his face and voice revealed this to even the most casual observer. He wrinkled his nose and forehead, curled his lip, gasped and then said, "Have you ever tried nutritional yeast?" Taking her cue from him, the patient replied, "No, and I don't want to!"

Another way to create resistance is by failing to take into account a per-son's MAP of reality on the subject, or trying to bypass these things like they are of no real consequence. And perhaps the most insidious way to create resistance is by projecting on your persuadee that they are resisting what you have to say. The feedback of resistance is a signal that you need to set your agenda aside, because there's something important that you've missed. Resistance is nature's way of saying 'Stop talking, start listening!'

Begin with the end in mind

The first question that a doctor is taught to ask a patient is, "What is your chief complaint?" more commonly expressed as "What's wrong?" or "What's your problem?" I've observed that everyone has the answer to those questions. Everyone knows what's wrong, what's the problem, and what is their chief complaint. Everybody knows what they don't want, including you. And complaining is easy, anyone can complain. But I can you what your problem is. The problem is that if all you know is what you don't want, you will get more of it. In part, this is the nature of sanity. And in part, it is a function of your reticular activating system, a group of cells in your brain stem that acts like radar for relevance to wants and don't wants.

Tell little Johnny not to 'bother those people,' and he will immediately proceed to do so. Tell little Johnny not to 'play with the cigarette butts in the ashtray,' and that's exactly what he'll do. The radar for relevance kicks in when you're getting married, and suddenly it seems the whole world is getting married too! Having a baby? It's a baby boom! Buying a certain car? There goes a truckload of them! What you notice is relevant to what you want, or don't want. And if all you know is what you don't want, you will get more of it.

That's why the challenge in life, and in the Art of Persuasion, is to define a direction, and organize yourself around that outcome. You need to know what you are aiming towards, what you intend to achieve, and why you intend to achieve it, or you just keep cycling back to the easy stuff, the complaints, problems, and obstacles that you can't seem to avoid.

Perhaps you've heard the expression, "Begin with the end in mind." Knowing what you intend to end up with is essential. I call this your persuasion proposition or proposal. It will help you organize, practice, and respond appropriately when the unexpected occurs. It is a fundamental key to purposeful and productive behavior.

A persuasion proposition consists of the following elements. What do you propose to do? (This is your idea, solution, product or service.) Who do you want to persuade to do it? Where do you intend for this to happen? When do you intend for this to happen? Why do you want to persuade your persuadee? And why should they care?

This last question, why should they care, is important, because people are more persuaded by their own interests than they are by yours.

People are persuaded by their own interests

Even if you know what's in it for them, you might as well be talking to a wall unless you know why they should care about it. And that's why a good deal of what you'll be reading in this book relates to understanding your persuadee. Why should they care about what you, the persuader, have to say?

It's time to take your first pass at a Persuasion Proposition. It's time to begin forming an actionable idea about the who, what, where, when and why of using the material in this book. Take some time and do this now. I'll wait here.

And you're back! First, let's review our useful assumptions.

You cannot not influence people.
Questions have persuasive power.
Flexibility increases persuasive power.
Resistance is a result.
People are persuaded by their own interests.
Begin with the end in mind.

Persuasion proposition in hand, and prepared with useful definitions and useful assumptions, it is now time to learn the persuasion dynamics upon which the art of persuasion depends!

3

STAGES OF CHANGE

James Prochaska, in his book 'Changing for Good,' offers a model that identifies five stages of change that people move through before a change is firmly entrenched in their lives.

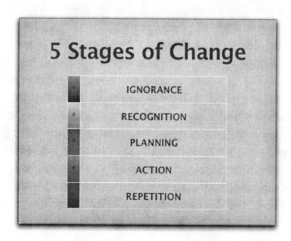

While his model was developed for working with people who have substance abuse problems, I find the model has a broader application that is both incredibly interesting and useful, and I have adapted it for our purposes of persuasion.

Stage one is IGNORANCE.

Ignorance is that state of mind where you don't know what you don't know. And sometimes, as the saying goes, ignorance is bliss. There is such a thing as willful ignorance, where a person intentionally ignores or refuses to pay attention to information that might cause cognitive dissonance or disturb their peace of mind. This is far more common than you might expect. Until you've presented your idea, insight or information, it is useful to assume that your persuadee is ignorant of it. This may not turn out to be true, so you want to pay attention for signals that they are farther along in their understanding than your initial assumption. The value of assuming ignorance is that it forces you not to get too far ahead of yourself, and serves as a reminder to speak clearly, carefully, and coherently in order to bring your persuadee to the next stage, recognition.

Ignorance is a delicate stage of change for introducing information, particularly if it is of the willful sort, and the right kind of information and delivery is required. For example, if your persuadee is ignorant of the consequences of his or her own behavior, you want to create a context of receptivity before introducing behaviorally specific information. Or maybe your persuadee knows about the problem behavior, and even the desired change, but is ignorant about how to go about acting on that knowledge. In that case, information has to be about options and methods. Or maybe your persuadee knows what the change is and how to go about it, but hasn't found the motivation to care. In that case, information should be motivational, that speaks to interests, values, and purpose.

I encourage you to assume your persuadee is ignorant about all of these possibilities until you know otherwise.

Stage Two is RECOGNITION

Recognition is that moment when it dawns on a person that there is something he can do and he wants to do it. He sees the light, and it beckons him on. The result of recognition is that he begins to seek out new information about options, opportunities and possibilities. You know that someone is at this stage if he starts asking questions about how to go forward.

This is a great moment, an AHA moment, a transformational moment. Suddenly, your persuadee realizes that a change is possible, or realizes that the method for a certain change is within his reach, or he realizes that there are very good reasons to care about making the desired change. If you listen well and provide the information he seeks, your persuadee moves on to the next stage.

Stage Three is PLANNING

Planning is the mentoring and modeling stage, where your helping hand is all that is required. In this stage, your persuadee begins to organize information for action, access resources, and plot a course. Your persuadee is getting ready for action.

Many failures of persuasion happen in this stage, because the preparation was inadequate for change. If change doesn't happen, that is not the time to jump to the worst conclusions (they didn't really mean it, they're incapable of change, etc.) but instead, recognize it as ignorance, restart the cycle to get recognition, then add what was missing into the next phase of the planning stage.

Stage Four is ACTION

With a plan in place, your persuadee is able to move forward, one step at a time. This is his chance to try on the change for size, to find out what happens, then learn from the experience and improve on it.

People need a lot of support in this stage. They need positive feedback that all is as it should be, and that change is definitely underway. Without this, people may lose heart, lose faith, give up, give in, and fall back to what is familiar territory. Don't be surprised if there are a few false starts at this stage, because when people try something new, things rarely go as expected. Action is the stage for offering reassurance and encouragement, giving support, helping your persuadee make sense of what's happening and fine tune his efforts. Reliable feedback is invaluable at this stage.

Doing something once doesn't guarantee that your persuadee's change is going to be set for the rest of their life. While beginning a change takes a lot more energy than sustaining it, nevertheless it takes energy and commitment to sustain a change. Otherwise, it is only a matter of time before a successful launch becomes a decaying orbit. You can't just walk away believing the situation is handled. Well, you can, but you'd be mistaken. Instead, you must go on to the fifth stage of Repetition.

Stage Five is REPETITION

For a new behavior to become habitual, it must be repeated repeatedly. For a new way of thinking to become habit, a person must think that way over and over again until the thought becomes firmly established. Human beings are creatures of habit, and habit is created through repetition and intensity. Until you can do it without even thinking about it, stage five must be considered to still be under way.

It is a mistake to expect people to go from ignorance to action in a single step. That kind of expectation is likely to introduce so much dissonance your persuadee's thinking that the natural impulse will be to deny, ignore or over-whelm the information with counterexamples in order to discharge the dissonance. The end result: Nothing changes, or change doesn't last.

Whenever you seek to persuade others, you can't leap from stage one to stage five, or even three. You move one stage at a time. So it's important to gauge at exactly which stage a person is at regarding the change you want to persuade them to make. Your goal is to move your persuadee to the next stage only. This will dramatically increase your success in persuasion.

No one goes from ignorance to habit in one move. Instead, don't push the river, as they say. Patience is truly a virtue. If someone is ignorant, your sole purpose is to introduce meaningful information, not to get a change. If they're in the recognition stage, all your efforts should focus on accessing resources and making a plan. If the person has a plan, all your efforts should be on getting them to take a step forward, to take some action, no matter how small. If they're taking action, then your focus must be on reinforcement. The Five Stages of Change is a powerful model for moving people from ignorance to habit.

POSSIBLE OUTCOMES

There are four possible ways for your persuasion interaction to turn out. When you attempt to persuade someone to change their mind, change their behavior, change their life, change their outfit, or change their opinion, two of these outcomes are worth your while, and two are opportunities to learn something about how you interact with others.

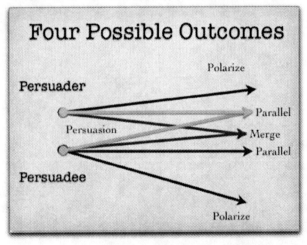

Parallel

You say to-may-to, I say to-mah-to, and we agree to disagree (or simply disagree.)

If the end of a persuasion interaction is just like the beginning, if nothing has changed, that is a 'PARALLEL' outcome. It is as if you both started out in one place, and ended up in the exact same place, with the same intentions, motivations, positions and understanding. This is what occurs when you fail to take into account the motivations and positions of your persuadee, and talk at them instead of with them. This all-too-common outcome is caused by a failure to listen first, or a failure to gain adequate understanding, or a failure to target what you've learned with what you have to say. It is, for the most part, completely avoidable.

Polarize

You say to-may-to, I say to-mah-to, and we both wish the tomatoes were rotten so we had something to throw at each other. Let's call the whole thing off!

The second possible outcome is that, as a result of your efforts, both you and your persuadee become more entrenched in your positions than you were before the interaction began. This is what happens when you contradict, argue, condescend, demand, ignore, attack, and otherwise send signals that you are right, your persuadee is wrong, and you have no idea what their dysfunction is. I call this a POLARIZED outcome, because both you and your persuadee end up farther apart than had you left well enough alone. If you've ever watched or listened to two people argue about politics, sex or religion, you know exactly what a polarized interaction looks, sounds and feels like.

Merge

I say to-may-to, you say to-mah-to, and we both realize that we're saying the same thing with a different accent! Let's enjoy whatever it is together!

The third possible outcome is what occurs when, as a result of your in-formation gathering and skill in persuasion, and your persuadee's information gathering and skill in persuasion, you both are persuaded to change your position or recognize the value of the other person's motivations, intentions and so on. This is a good outcome. Any time you can get this outcome, chalk it up as progress and be grateful for it. Using the skills offered in this book should easily lead to this outcome in almost every situation where you seek to persuade. I call it the MERGE, where your interests and your persuadee's interests are met, where your motivations and your persuadee's motivations are valued, where both you and your persuadee yield some of the territory surrounding your position. Way to go! Terrific!

Persuade

I say to-may-to, and you say, ok, to-may-to it is.

The fourth outcome, and the one you probably had in mind when you began reading this book, is what happens when your persuadee comes around to your point of view, where your intentions become their intentions, your position becomes their position, your motivation becomes their motivation. This is rare and unusual, but not impossible. In fact, using the information in this book, your ability to get this outcome will increase. I call this outcome PERFECT PERSUASION.

5

THE ACCEPTANCE ZONE

To persuade with integrity, you must first seek not to persuade, but to build a relationship on trust. To achieve the result of greater trust, you must be trust worthy. And to be trust worthy, you must have your persuadee's best interests (as they understand them, not as you desire them!) in your mind, your heart and in your actions. The beauty of such an approach is that trust leads to acceptance. Working only for your own interests, even when you deem it in their interest, undermines your persuasive potential, by leading to distrust and rejection. And once you've been rejected, you have compounded your difficulty dramatically.

Three receiving zones

Consider that there are three ways that what you say can be received, three zones in the mind of your persuadee that represent various degrees of receptivity, Acceptance, Rejection, and Uncommitted (i.e., I don't care.) The Acceptance zone contains the MAP and other information held as 'the reality' by your persuadee. Your information will be filtered through your persuadee's MAP into one of the three zones, just as soon as you present it. Your ability to persuade depends on closely targeting that MAP with what you say when you speak.

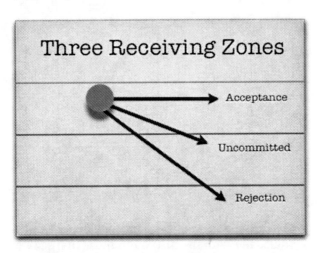

Obviously, accepting your persuadee's MAP is the fastest way into the Acceptance Zone. But then, no persuasion would occur. The good news is that all around that MAP are similar or related ideas of reality that your persuadee can find acceptable. You don't have to share your persuadee's personal reality to be persuasive, but the closer you are to it when you begin to speak, the more persuasive you are going to be. It's not about staying there (which is what happens when YOU are persuaded,) just starting there.

Your success with persuasion depends on your acceptance of the following useful assumption: Every person accepts their own version of reality as 'the reality,' or at least prefers it to all other versions. The acceptance zone is where each person's idea of reality resides. Your ability to persuade depends on closely targeting that idea of reality with what you say in the first moment that you speak. You don't have to agree with their exact version of reality, but you do have to come close to it or you run the risk of your words landing in their REJECTION ZONE. And the unconscious decision to accept or reject what you say will take place almost immediately.

Meet them where they are

That's the bad news. Acceptance or rejection happens fast, and once your words have been rejected, you will find it far more challenging to be persuasive. But there's plenty of good news here that will make this idea easier for you to accept. It turns out that there are an infinite number of possible realities, in whole or in part, surrounding a person's idea of reality as relates to your ideas and information, that the person can find acceptable.

So you don't have to share their personal reality to be persuasive, but you have to speak to it in a familiar way, so that your persuadee recognizes himself or herself in what you say. The closer you are to their understanding of their own needs and interests when you begin to speak, the more persuasive you are going to be. It's not about staying there (which is what happens when YOU are persuaded), just starting there.

More good news! Even if what you say lands outside of their ACCEPTANCE ZONE, there's the possibility that it will wind up in the I DON'T CARE ZONE, which is a better place to land than outright rejection.

Let's review. People quickly place incoming information into 1 of 3 zones, all in relationship to their MAP of reality. Acceptance. Rejection. I don't care. And this is why it is so important to know something about the person or group to whom you intend to speak persuasively. Because the closer you are to their MAP when you begin, the more persuasive you are going to be.

If you offer information or ideas that are rejected, you won't be very persuasive, because rejection makes persuasion highly unlikely. The two other zones give you a much better chance. Each zone contains all the related MAPS for that particular subject, idea or information. What is acceptable, what is un-acceptable, and whatever.

If you want people to accept change, you need to invest some time in planning and communication. All too often, managers and colleagues (or parents and spouses, for that matter) just throw a change out there and expect others to say, "Well, that's just fine." Such people are living in a fantasy world. To get people to accept change, the first step is to understand what, from their perspective, they have to gain by changing, or stand to lose by staying the same.

Sometimes, size matters

It is easier to influence someone to be in favor of something, or at least go along with something, when they have a large zone of acceptance. So what affects the size of the Acceptance Zone? The importance of the issue or idea to the individual's or group's self-identity and self-definition. The more invested a person is on any given issue, the larger the zone of Rejection and the smaller the zone of Acceptance. Common sense, isn't it? Think about it. If something is important to you, you've already done a lot of thinking about it and decided where you are at in relationship to it. Truth is on your side. Anyone addressing you about it is either going to be with you or against you.

Conversely, the less invested in their MAP of reality, the larger the zone of Acceptance. But if your presentation is too much at variance with the MAP of your persuadee, no matter how big the zone of Acceptance, you will miss it. And if you seem to be diametrically opposed to their MAP of reality, your op-position guarantees their opposition. So it behooves you, when you seek to persuade, to start by narrowly targeting their MAP, and then working your way out from there. There is, however, one significant exception to what I just told you. If a person already has enough trust in you, they may quickly let go of their personal reality in favor of the one you offer. And that's why building trust is JOB NUMBER ONE. And how do we do that? By blending.

Trust me on this, the next chapter will open your eyes and change your life!

6

BLEND TO BUILD TRUST

Trust Building is Job Number One

All the flexibility and direction in the world won't help your persuasion efforts if you lack trust. But if a person has enough trust in you, they may quickly let go of their personal reality in favor of the one you offer. Building trust is essential. And how do we do that? By blending.

All the other skills and strategies in this book depend on blending to be effective. You already know how to blend. But if you don't know how to do it on purpose, it's likely to be the last thing you think of when you most need to do it! I realize that saying you already know how to do it is a huge assumption. So here's a test. Do you have at least one friend? If you do, you know how to blend. If you don't, you're about to find out what's been missing in your life.

Since blending is such a powerful persuader, let us define terms. Blending is the means by which you reduce differences between yourself and others. Said another way, blending means that you send signals of similarity. It's what you do automatically with your friends when you share experiences. It's what happens when people share a vision or agree to a mission. You've heard of it this way. 'Birds of a feather flock together.' Fact is, we the people like people who are, in some way, like us.

Basic Rule

The irony of conflict is that everybody has more in common with everyone else than they have differences. But instead of emphasizing the similarities in policies, plans and relations, the differences get all the attention. The result is that everybody who fixates on differences winds up in the rejection zone, and nobody walks away happy. Oh well. There's a choice to be made here, and blending is the choice. The basic rule of persuasion is this: Nobody cooperates with anybody who seems to be against them.

The key words in this rule are 'seems to be.' You don't have to be against someone for them to think that you are. But in human relationships, there is no middle ground. In every interaction, every person, first and foremost, looks and listens for an answer to one. "Are you with me or not?" And if you're not with them, if you're neutral, or more focused on yourself than you are on them, you run the risk of coming across as against them. So learn this rule and learn it well. Say it with me now: Nobody cooperates with anybody who seems to be against them. Get it? Got it? Good!

How do we send signals of similarity to let people know we are on their side? Telling them is not enough. The signals of similarity get sent through body posture, animation, facial expressions, voice volume and tempo, need-style, and lastly, through our words.

55, 38, 7

In 1967, Dr. Albert Mehrabian conducted an interesting study at the University of California in Los Angeles. He wanted to understand how people make sense out of mixed messages, particularly when there is emotion involved. He concluded that 55% of the meaning made is based on what the person appears to be saying, the visual component of communication. 38% of the meaning made is based on what it sounds like the person is saying. And only 7% of the meaning made is based on the words that a person uses. In other words, 93% of the meaning made is based on how something is said, rather than what is said.

I had an experience years ago that drove this home for me. I had stopped for a cup of coffee at a convenience store. Now, my mother brought me up to be nice to people for no particular reason. So when I walked in to the store, I smiled at the guy behind the counter and said good morning. He was apparently not brought up by my mother, because instead of a friendly smile back, all I got was a scowl and a grumble. Fair enough. No harm, no foul, on to the subject at hand. "Where's the coffee?" I asked pleasantly. "Over there!" he said pointedly, as he pointed to the back right corner of the store. I comforted myself with the thought that at least he knew where it was! I walked to the back of the store, and poured myself some coffee. Then I looked around for a little milk, cream, or half and half. But all I found was a container of non-dairy creamer. I confess, I don't care for non-dairy creamer, no, not at all.

"Excuse me," said I, as politely as I could. "I hate non-dairy creamer, don't you?" I had hoped to gain some agreement, but instead he said, "I like it," in a way that sounded like a putdown of me! But full speed ahead, I continued. "Oh well. Say, do you have any dairy products I could use for my coffee in-stead?" "No," he replied with absolute certainty. Undaunted, I looked around to see if there was anything I could substitute for their milk substitute. And that's when I saw it. A cooler, near the cash register, containing 14 flavors of ice cream. "Mmmm," I thought to myself. "Ice cream would do nicely." I picked out a flavor, and turned to the clerk. "Would it be possible," I began tentatively, "to get a spoonful of ice cream in my coffee?" He didn't miss a beat. "NO!" Hmmm, this wasn't going so well. Maybe if I offered to compromise, he might move from his position a little bit. "Fair enough. How about a half a spoonful?" I smiled. He snarled, and then spit out each word. "I.....SAID....NO!!!"

Let's review. Did I know what I wanted? (Begin with the end in mind.) Yes. Was I being flexible? Yes. I offered new solutions, and I offered a compromise. Then what's missing from this picture? The creamer!!! Actually, the missing ingredient was blending. My behavior, while polite and pleasant in my reality, was abrasive and aggravating in his! For this story to have a happy ending, I needed to try a little blending. I set down the cup of coffee. Why? To reduce the differences between us (He wasn't holding one!) I folded my arms like him. I put my left foot out further than my right foot, just like him. I even made my face look a little like his, which was no easy task. And in a voice that was a little less aggressive than his, but certainly assertive, I said, "Look! Is this something I did, or are you just having a rough day?" And magic happened. He turned and began to account for his behavior. "The night shift leaves me their mess, and I've got to clean it up." He shrugged. "What flavor?" Yes, that's what he said! And I replied "Chocolate Chip."

Blending changes everything. It tells people that you are with them instead of against them. And it increases the likelihood of cooperation instead of conflict. Are you with me? Are you? Because if you are with me, I can tell you a number of simple ways to blend with others.

37

55% - Body Posture, Animation and Expression

Let's start with the 55%, the visible component of interpersonal communication. For our purposes, we're talking about body posture, animation and facial expressions. Blending reveals that if your persuadee is sitting and you are standing, you should sit down. If they are standing and you are sitting, you should either stand up or offer them a chair. Blending reveals that if they cross their legs and you fold your arms, you are sending a signal of similarity. You don't want to do everything that your persuadee is doing, because you don't want to create an identity crisis, as in "If you're me, who am I?" But you can notice what they are doing with their body posture, and mirror some of it back.

Animation level refers to the fact that some people are more animated communicators than others. Some people talk with their hands, for example, while others just talk with their mouths. Captain Kirk uses his entire body to emphasize every word, while Mr. Spock has a single eyebrow that gets involved whenever he listens or talks. Blending reveals that if your persuadee is an animated communicator, then you'll want to be at least a little animated in your communications with him. And if your persuadee is not particular animated and you are, you'll want to tone down your behavior. After all, it is hard for the nonanimated communicator to hear what a person is saying when they're pre-occupied with watching the other person's hands, arms and face move around.

Our facial expressions tell people all kinds of things, and not always what we intend. Have you ever smiled at someone that didn't smile back? Remember your reaction to that? Chances are, you felt a little offended! "I'll never smile at them again!" Ever been in pain and somebody stood there grinning at you? I think that's what we call 'customer service,' right? The point is, if someone is not smiling and you are, and you want to be persuasive, a signal of similarity gets sent when you wipe that goofy smile off your face. And if you're having a tough day and your persuadee isn't, at least account for your behavior so they don't take it personally. "Sorry, I'm having a rough day." Then your face won't distract them from hearing your words.

38% - Voice Tempo and Volume

This brings us to the 38% of communication. Some people talk fast. Some people talk slow. You'll know you're going too fast if you find yourself having this thought. "How many times do I have to say this?" If you want the answer to be 'one more' you've got to slow it down. You'll know you're taking too long if people start squirming while you talk, or claw their way out of the room. Fast talkers often treat slow talkers rudely, because fast talkers find it rude of slow talkers to take so much time to finish their sentences. Fast talkers even fill in the blanks to help slow talkers along, and so they can get back to their lives sooner. Blending reveals the importance of noticing the pace at which another person speaks, and then matching that pace in order to seem similar. Do you have to talk as fast or slow as another person? No. But you want to reduce the differences and send signals of similarity.

Have you ever had somebody stand 3 inches away from you and shout, "How are you doing?" so loudly that you have to shove your finger in your ear and stir it around before you reply, "Well, something just broke, so the answer is different already!" Have you ever tried to get information from somebody mumbling in a loud environment? You say "What?" and they are always nice enough to repeat themselves. You repeat "What?" and they're always nice enough to repeat themselves again. And you think, "What's the problem?" and the answer is, you need to blend. That means, believe it or not, that sometimes you have to mumble back. When you do, a funny thing happens. They say "What?" which is your cue to blend, by saying "I know! I'm having trouble hearing you in here too!" at which point they completely get the problem and voluntarily begin speaking up so you can hear them.

That's the power of blending. It gives you a behavioral approach to increasing cooperation and trust. And all that's required of you is to pay attention to the person you are communicating with, and send them a few signals of similarity, so they'll know you are on their side.

There's another element with which you can blend, and it comes through in the way a person talks. Meet me in the next chapter to learn about need-styles, and how you can use this model to build trust and cooperation.

7

BLEND WITH NEED-STYLE

The way a person structures their communication gives you valuable information about how to structure your communication in response. You can recognize communication needs by noticing communication style.

Before I can tell you about need-styles, I need you to make an important distinction between behavior and personality. I want you to avoid the trap of putting people into personality boxes and then treating them like your box is their personality. Why is it a trap? Because personality is a generalization, based on limited information. Behavior changes, depending on variables in the communication environment. People have a variety of behaviors to draw on, depending on who they're with, what's going on, and most importantly, what's important to them at any particular moment in time.

I'm sure you've heard the saying, 'Think outside the box." Here's my version of that. "Don't get in the box in

41

the first place." In this chapter, I'm going to share with you a model for quickly hearing what a person needs in their interactions with you. It is not based on personality types. It is based on behavior, and because behavior changes, you are required to keep paying attention in order to notice those changes.

There are four styles in particular that reflect four communication needs. You can blend with these styles in order to speak to these needs. How many? Four.

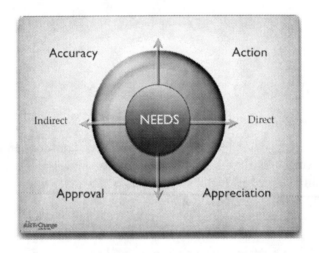

To recognize a person's need-style, you've got to notice what they talk about and how directly they talk about it. Sometimes, people talk more about what they're doing. That means they are focused on a task, whether the task is discussing an idea, making a decision, resolving a dispute or achieving an objective. We'll call that a 'task focus. ' Sometimes, people talk more about the people around them, or their feelings in a given situation. We'll call that a people focus.

A person focused more on a task than on people may pay more attention to the end result of the task than the details they encounter along the way. Or, they may pay more attention to the details of the task than to the end result. You can notice this in the way they talk. A person focused more on people than on a task may express more interest in the opinions and feelings of others, or in their own opinions and feelings.

Need for action

When a person is focused on the end result of an interaction or an idea, he has a communication need for action. She needs you to speak directly and actively. She needs to hear movement in a direction in the way you talk.

Need for accuracy

When a person is focused on the details of an interaction or an idea, she has a communication need for accuracy. She needs to hear that you are paying attention to the details in the way you talk.

Need for approval

When a person is focused more on what others think and say than on her own thoughts and feelings, she has a need for approval. She needs to hear that you also have a concern for the thoughts and feelings of others in the way you talk.

Need for appreciation

When a person is focused more on her own thoughts and feelings than the thoughts and feelings of others, she has a need for appreciation. She needs to hear that you appreciate her in the way you talk.

These needs, action, accuracy, approval and appreciation, get communicated through the style or structure by which a person speaks. And there are indicators, when you notice them, that allow you to *speak to the need*.

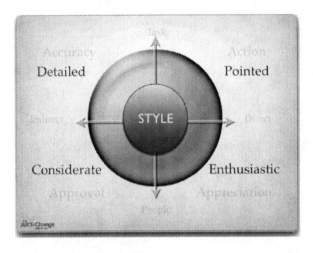

Action = Get to the point

The person with a need for action will speak directly, and to the point. There's no mincing of words here, as momentum and movement are of a high priority. "Just do it." She is likely to speak in a commanding and authoritative manner. Blending reveals that when a person is direct and to the point, you want to be direct and to the point in dealing with her.

Accuracy = Give the details

The person with a need for accuracy will speak indirectly, offer a lot of detail, and take her time before arriving at the point. You may find yourself wondering about the point of it, but eventually she'll get there. "It is, perhaps, potentially important to take into consideration a variety of options and possibilities before drawing a conclusion that might prove erroneous over time. Therefore, after careful consideration, and having thoroughly examined all possibilities, one is left with the idea that perhaps we ought to do it." When accuracy is important, she is likely to ask questions to acquire information, or make long statements to establish facts and stimulate thinking. Blending reveals that when a person is indirect and detailed, you want to be indirect and detailed in your communications with her.

Approval = Be friendly and considerate

The person with a need for approval will speak indirectly, and express concern for the opinions and feelings of others, constantly checking back to avoid giving offense, and she will be sensitive to the other person's needs and have great respect for their time. "Is this a good time? Would you like me to come back later? Yes? No? You tell me, I'll understand. Do you think we should do it? Never mind, I'm sorry to have bothered you, I'll just do it myself," Blending reveals that when a person is indirect and talks in a considerate manner, you want to be indirect and considerate in your communications with her.

Appreciation = Energy and enthusiasm

The person with a need for appreciation will speak directly and enthusiastically, using exclamations and personal stories to grab attention and evoke feelings, in order to hold the spotlight of your attention (and by inference, your appreciation for what they have to say.) "I feel that we ought to do this, and I'll tell you why. I've given this a lot of thought, because it's important to me. And it ought to be important to you, too, because after all, there's a time and a place for it, and this is that time, and this is that place." And you may be wondering why they're going on and on about it, but blending reveals that when a person is direct and enthusiastic, you want to be direct and enthusiastic in your communications with her.

Once you hear where someone is coming from, you have a vector of approach for your persuasion efforts. When dealing with action-focused communication, just cut to the chase. When dealing with accuracy driven communication, go step by step, and do not require any leaps of faith. When dealing with approval seeking communication, be considerate and patient, and use relation-ship language, like 'we,' 'us,' 'you and me,' and 'the team.' When dealing with appreciation-centered communication, use acknowledgement and enthusiasm to create a spotlight effect with your words.

How can you apply this in your persuasion efforts? I think it's a good idea to practice delivering your persuasion proposition using all four of these communication need-styles. Then you will be prepared for any of them. Do this now, before meeting me in the next chapter.

LISTEN TO GO DEEP

Three Phases of Persuasion

We've set in place our useful definitions and useful assumptions. We've explored the persuasion dynamics of stages of change, possible outcomes and receiving zones. We've investigated the power of blending in trust building. We've described how to hear a person's communication needs through the style by which they structure their communication. Now is the time to talk about the words that people use to describe their experience, that 7% of meaning upon which the 93% depends.

All persuasion interactions, whether parenting, cold calls, speeches and training programs, proposals, decisions and resolutions go through three phases. First is listening. Then transitioning. And lastly, talking. Listening has to precede talking, because listening is how you discover why someone will care about your persuasion proposition. From this point on, we will move through each phase in turn. This is our first chapter about listening.

Words are symbols for experience. Like the proverbial iceberg, words have a surface structure that is just the tip of meaning, and a massive deep structure of meaning behind

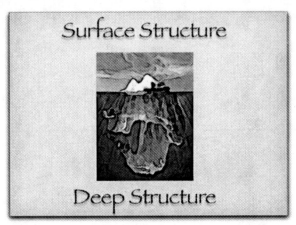

them. And we can get to that deeper meaning by acknowledging the words people use, and then using those same words to convey commonality.

I'm about to share with you the first of three listening strategies that can take you from the surface to the deep. These listening strategies are based on three useful assumptions about the power of listening.

Three useful assumptions about listening

1. When people talk, they want to be heard and understood.

2. People actually like to hear themselves talk, even when they are complaining or angry.

3. People are drawn to people who listen to them talk.

"One of the best ways to persuade others is with your ears-
by listening to them." Dean Rusk

Listening is a fantastic way to find out what you need to know in order to target your words at another person's Acceptance Zone.

Three good reasons to listen

1. Information is power.

2. Most people don't know what they're talking about unless someone asks them.

3. You can draw people towards your persuasion proposition with questions.

Do you always know exactly what you mean when you start talking? Have you ever wondered why you cared about something? Were you ever surprised at the direction a conversation took? Has anyone ever gotten upset with you because what he or she heard was different than what you said? Let's explore listening as a powerful tool to gain access to the acceptance zone.

Look and sound like you understand

When you listen to people talk, the first words you hear just scratch the surface the thoughts and attitudes they represent, and tell you very little of what the person means in choosing those words. Yet the wise listener knows that it is helpful to both of you to give the appearance of understanding in order to find the deeper meaning.

For example, if I tell you that, "I like fish," do you know what I mean? Without more information, all you can know is what those particular words mean to you, not to me.

And that's why you want to listen actively when I say those words, "I like fish."

To gain a deeper understanding, look and sound like you know exactly what I mean, while knowing that you don't know. Then say my words back to me, and ask questions about them, because questions open up opportunities for persuasion.

When I tell you that I like fish, you can nod your head as if you completely understand, while knowing that you don't know what I mean. You can grunt affirmatively every once in a while when I talk, so that it sounds like you know exactly what I mean, all the while knowing that you don't know what I mean. You can even say back some of what I say to you. That's called backtracking, and it is yet another way of sounding like you completely understand, while knowing that you don't know what I mean.

Look confused when asking questions

Now, at this point you may wonder at what point you get to look confused, since you don't actually know what I mean when I say "I like fish." And the answer is, you get to look confused whenever you are asking a question. When others are talking, you look sound and speak like you completely understand. When you ask a question, you get to look confused. Get it? Got it? Good. But you don't want your persuadee to be confused by your questions. So you always backtrack before asking a question. Always? Yes. If your intent is to persuade, always backtrack be-fore asking a question.

What questions? Yes.

But what kind of questions should you ask? The idea is to ask open-ended questions that require more than a grunt in response.   Instead of "do you, did you, are you, will you," and a host of other closed questions that require only a yes/no or grunt in response, you want to ask questions that are open ended, that require information, in order to get to the deeper meaning.   And open ended questions always begin with who, what, where, when and how (and why, but not yet!)

Why not why?

Are you wondering why I said why, but not yet? Isn't why an open-ended question that you get to ask while looking confused? Here's why. Most people don't actually know what they're talking about. If you ask them why they are talking about it, you confuse them and they start making stuff up! There is a time and a place for wy, but not yet.

OK, let's review the basic listening strategy.   First, you look like you understand (nod your head), and sound like you understand (grunt and utter affirming phrases like 'yes, mmhmm, I see'), and talk like you understand (backtracking the same words that you heard without adding any new ones.) You blend by nodding, grunting and backtracking, and then ask questions that begin with what, who, where, when and how.   Always backtrack before asking questions.   And that is how you go deeper to get higher quality information in the least amount of time.

The best listening seeks to get to deep structure information, rather than divert away from it with the listener's own thoughts, words, and ideas.   But sometimes people say confusing things.   Your tendency in that moment might be to try and figure it out.   But figuring it out is pointless, because you can't.   They said it, and they know more about what it means than you do.

So if you are ever at a loss for words because you are uncertain as to what question to ask, or distracted by something that the person you are listening to said or did, or you are just plain lost in the jungle of their words, then the fastest way to go deeper is to say, straight up, the intention behind your questions. And you do that by saying these words. "Tell me more!" The deep structure meaning of words is best left to the person who offered those words. Instead of hallucinating freely, allow yourself to feel confused. But don't curse the darkness. Turn on the searchlight of "Tell me more!" to find your way deeper into the other person's meaning.

Is listening in the way I've described always necessary? No. There's a time and a place for everything, and it's never all the time and every place. But remember, information is power. The more you know, the easier it will be to target the Acceptance Zone.

Listen to emotion

Though you cannot reason with an upset person, you can get an upset person to become reasonable. Look like, sound like, and talk like their emotional language makes all the sense in the world. Then ask a question, and continue to backtrack and ask another question after that, until you have the who, the what, the where, the when and the how of it. Why does this work? Because when a person is upset, their brain isn't connected to their mouth. Instead, their stress is doing the talking. By listening actively, you influence them to find their brain and start making sense. They become reasonable, as you become persuasive.

Listen when you suspect a hidden agenda

If there is a hidden agenda, the last thing you want the person to do is work harder at hiding it. Instead, listen actively in the manner I've recommended here, and you will eventually tease the agenda out of the deep structure.

Listen when you suspect someone is lying

If you suspect a lie and say your suspicion out loud, a lying person will work harder at concealing a lie. Listen as I've described, and a lying person will wind up spilling the beans. They won't mean to, it just happens. Want proof? Rent a Columbo video!

Listen when you think it is a bad idea

Listening in the way I've described in this chapter can be particularly powerful when dealing with people who seem to think they know everything. (Certain teenagers, parents, and bosses fit easily under this label.) If you tell someone he has a bad idea, his polarity response to your criticism pretty much guarantees that he will have to act on his bad idea just to prove you wrong.

But if, instead of opposing him, you look and sound and talk like what you're hearing makes all the sense in the world, and then ask a question that reveals the badness of the idea, like "And how will you pay for that?" or, "How am I supposed to do that?" Or, "How do you know that this won't worsen the problem?" you'll spare both of you the cost of acting on a bad idea.

Listen when dealing with criticism

How do you react to criticism? Do you like it? Most people don't care for it, not even a little. And it's not uncommon to have a knee jerk reaction and defend oneself against it. The problem with defending against criticism is best summed up in a phrase mistakenly attributed to William Shakespeare: "Methinks thou doest protest too much!" When you defend against criticism, you wind up looking and sounding guiltier than had you said nothing at all.

On the other hand, when you listen in the manner I've described in this chapter, you will get one of three outcomes, any one of which is, I think, a positive outcome.

1. The critical person will realize it isn't really about you.

2. You will learn something valuable for dealing with that person.

3. You take the pleasure out of it and the person just stops doing it.

Soon, you'll learn how to go even deeper. You may be wondering, at this point, "Is there ever a time for close-ended questions like 'Do you, did you, have you ever?" The answer is yes. There is a time. We'll discuss the use of close-ended questions later. For now, go listen to the people around you and go deeper than the surface of what they say. Then meet me in the next chapter.

9

FIND THE MAP: MOTIVATION

In this chapter, we'll begin an adventure that will take us deep into the territory of your persuadee's internal workings. Then I'll share with you a truly *big idea* that can make a tremendous difference in your persuasive power, *if* you have the desire to learn it and use it. I'm going to ask and then answer some important questions regarding motivation. For example, what is motivation? Motivation is an incentive, an inducement, or a stimulus for action. In other words, it is anything - verbal, physical, or psychological - that causes somebody to do something in response.

Why do people change their minds? What makes a person care about one thing more than another? What is their motivation? How can you find out?

It's in the MAP

The MAP to a person's personal reality consists of their Motivation, Access Language and Position. Your mission, when listening to others, is to go deep and FIND THE MAP! In this chapter, we'll explore the first of three key aspects of the deep structure MAP behind your persuadee's actions and decisions, motivation!

You can't motivate other people. But you can help people find their motivation. You can speak to motivation and engage people at a deep level, and bring about change as a result. Drive and determination, inhibition and restraint are the consequences of motivation, because motivation is all about the direction of our motion or movement in life, either towards or away. Motivation is context specific. It changes, like so many details about how we live our lives; depending on the situation we're in, the people involved, and our priorities at that moment in time.

Your motivation to do or not do something can often be found in the answer, or lack of an answer, to the question 'What's in it for me?' That's true about everyone else, too. Everybody is interested in what's in it for him or her, no matter what it is. The art of persuasion is about getting people to do something because they want to do it, not because you want them to do it. You've got to find out what they really want, and then help them understand how your proposition helps them get it. Perhaps the simplest way to understand motivation is to divide it into two motivations: Fear and Desire.

Fear and Desire

Some people are driven to action by the desire for something. Desire pulls them forward. You can hear the sound of desire when people describe moving toward their goals, toward their values, toward a reward, toward a challenge, toward fulfillment, toward personal worth, and toward pleasure of any kind. Desire is a strong motivational force with long lasting effects

56

Sometimes, people are motivated more by fear than by desire. When they do go forward, it's because they're trying to get away from something. And when they stand still and take no action, it is usually because they are holding themselves back in order to avoid something. Avoid problems. Stay away from consequences. Get away from failure, worthlessness and pain. You can hear when fear is the motivation, because people talk about what they don't want, or want to avoid, or how they want to get as much distance as possible from something they deem undesirable.

There's no denying that fear gets our interest, and holds it, at least for a little while. Our entire nervous system is designed to be afraid in a heartbeat, and it often goes off without warning. It also gets our interest when people tell us we have reason to fear. Our nervous system responds by wanting to fight or get away. That's why the oldest trick in the persuasion deck is to really scare someone, and then offer them an easy solution that eliminates the threat. It's practically guaranteed, at least in the short term, to generate interest and engage motivation. For example, in the two weeks following a speeding ticket, a driver will typically behave better on the road. But it doesn't take long for the old habit of behavior to kick in. Fear is insufficient as a long-term motivator for change.

You must walk a fine and fearful line to use fear as a motivator. Apply too little, and it won't gain any interest. Apply too much, and you overload and exhaust the receptors for it, with the paradoxical effect of losing interest. Even if the amount is just right, you have to keep using it to keep people interested. While fear plays an important role in motivation, it cannot create sustained motivation by itself.

Desire is a much more powerful long-term motivator. Desire beckons calls us forward and beckons us onward. Desire pulls us out of ourselves and into meaningful action. If you know exactly why you want to do something, doing it is no big deal. If you know why something matters to you, doing something about it is the natural response. And when you add in a little fear to a lot of desire, you have strong reasons to go forward both in front of you and behind.

Maslow's Hierarchy

There have been many studies and numerous models developed to account for the drivers in human behavior. One well-known model is Maslow's Hierarchy of Needs.

According to this model, meeting our baseline needs as human beings is the prime motivation. It is an imperative that compels us to attend to our bodies, by seeking food, warmth, shelter, sleep, and sex. When these needs are unmet, nothing else matters.

Once these needs are met, we focus on safety, keeping ourselves safe from harm. We seek protection and security, either through the accumulation of power, or surrounding ourselves with people

Once we feel safe, a need to belong to something greater than ourselves emerges. We join a group, become part of a tribe, work and play together with others in order to share a sense of belonging.

Once we belong, our need for status kicks in. We take on responsibility, and work to gain the respect and esteem of others.

Once all these needs are met, biological, safety, belonging and esteem, we are freed from our struggle to find our place in the world. Now our needs shift inwards. We find the motivation to first know and then become what we are capable of becoming, through the pursuit of happiness and personal fulfillment.

McClelland's Motivational Model

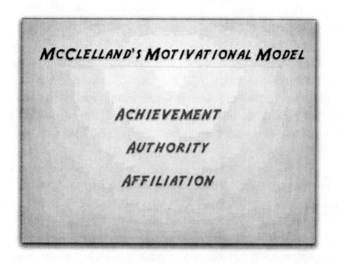

David McClelland developed another model while teaching at Harvard. He sought to understand the motivations of people in the workplace. In his 1988 book, Human Motivation, he identified three kinds of motivational needs: achievement, authority and affiliation. McClelland believed that each of us exhibits some combination of these 3 motivations in our work.

A person motivated by the need for achievement seeks opportunities for advancement, and works to attain challenging goals. Such a person is open to, and seeks out, feedback about their progress and successes. McClelland felt that this motivation has the potential to produce the best workplace leaders, unless those leaders fall into the trap of asking too much of others in the mistaken belief that everyone shares this motivation.

A person motivated by the need for authority seeks opportunities for influence, status and prestige. They have a strong work ethic and make strong commitments. They know they can count on themselves to follow through. McClelland believed that this need for authority motivates a person to take charge. Their downfall is getting attached to an idea, or lacking the skills to get others to act.

A person motivated by the need for affiliation wants to be liked, and works really hard at it. Considered by some as the ideal team player, such a person is generally appreciated by many, and disliked by only a few. Their downfall is that the need to be liked gets in the way of decisive action.

Clearly, there are differences in these models. And there are many other motivational models. I think that sometimes it is more valuable to set our models aside and just ask a person, "Why do you care about that?" Yet I'm motivated to have a model that accounts for motivation in a way that helps with persuasion. Since I couldn't find such a model anywhere, I decided to develop my own. It's based on the idea that we are motivated towards or away, because of desire or fear. I call it Kirschner's Motivational Model.

Maybe this is a status move on my part, but I don't think so. I offer it to you not just because it is in your interest that I do so (authority,) but the fact is that I put a lot of time, thought and energy into its development (achievement) and I think you'll really like it (affiliation.) If you're hungry for more information, and you feel safe enough to continue, and think you'll fit in better and be more worthy and want to fulfill your persuasive potential, you're going to love this model! So leaving McClelland and Maslow behind, let us examine my motivational model and find out if it can help you be more persuasive.

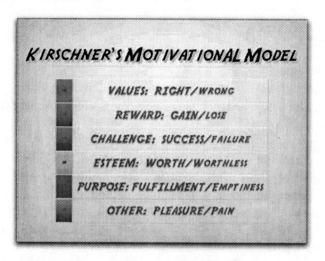

Kirschner Motivational Model

According to the Kirschner model, there are six motivational sets, each with a TOWARDS side and an AWAY side. These sets play an important role in the choices people make, and they give us some leverage with the art of persuasion.

Values

Some people are motivated to take action because they believe it is the right thing to do, or not take action because they are certain it is wrong to do so. The issues of morality and politics give us a place to test our values, and a conflict of values is often found at the heart of the most divisive issues we face in modern society.

It is next to impossible to persuade a person motivated by their values to go along with something they perceive as 'wrong.' Values are also often a significant element of society, because they are a part of the shared rules of the tribe. Values are tripwires for persuaders, so it is always important to know something of your persuadee's values.

Reward

Some people are moved to act when there is something to gain or something to lose. This motivation gives birth to incentive programs, contests, perks and prizes, sales and bonuses.

Some rewards are extrinsic, in that you find them outside of yourself, like the little sound of pleasure a person makes when you give them a gift or do something that he or she enjoys. Other rewards are internal (intrinsic.) You find them in yourself, because the journey is the reward. Rewards must work, because you generally can expect to get what you reward, and things that get rewarded get done. Intrinsic rewards are more motivating than extrinsic ones. And rewards for doing nothing tend to reinforce doing nothing. So be careful about what you reward.

Challenge

Some people are thrilled by the chance to succeed, or terrified at the risk of failure. The challenge motivation is behind much of athletic and academic achievement, business building, political action and artistic endeavor. And some people will eagerly take up a challenge as a group that they wouldn't touch on their own, because of perceived safety in numbers, the availability of support and encouragement, and people to pick up the slack if someone can't quite measure up.

The reverse is also true. Some people will eagerly take up a challenge on their own, but wouldn't dream of doing it with a group, because of concern about meddling and interference. Under the right conditions, almost anyone can be challenged effectively to meet a challenge.

What leads to success when taking on a challenge? You've got to have some vision, and passion to realize it. You've got to follow through with goals and planning. Then you'll need perseverance, courage and integrity to stay the course. That's how you meet a challenge. What leads to failure? People fail due to a lack of vision and passion, a lack of preparation, and a lack of perseverance. Do the math and add it all up, and the path to success or failure in meeting any challenge is clear. And attending to these details makes a challenge more enticing and persuasive.

Esteem

Some people just want to be acknowledged as worthy, and go to great lengths to prove it. This motivation produces a desire to be somebody, to achieve something, and to receive public praise for it. Other people have a great sense of worthlessness. It makes them defensive and they go to great lengths to avoid being singled out for criticism. Many family problems stem from this motivation.

The Esteem set is the domain of good and bad reputations, of fame and shame, respect and disdain, honor and dishonor. Esteem is enhanced through recognition, which is sometimes called the oxygen of motivation. Mary Kay Ash, founder of Mary Kay Cosmetics, famously said that people want only two things more than sex and money, and that's recognition and praise. She believed in 'praising people to success.' When you consider the empire she built and the pink Cadillac awards associated with her brand, it becomes apparent that she used this motivation to great advantage.

Purpose

Some people have a cause in which they believe which gives them a chance to find fulfillment, or at least escape from the emptiness they fear. The motive of purpose exists beyond material benefit, beyond compensation, beyond reward. Purpose is the big reason why.

Our relationships give our lives purpose. We do it for the children. We do it for the community. We do it for our country. We do it to leave a legacy, or make our mark in history. And for those whose lives lack such meaning, we do it in hopes of finding meaning and filling the emptiness inside.

Other

I think a great model has to leave some room for 'other.' And in this case, it seems that most other motivations fall into the set of pleasure and pain.

Some people are motivated to seek pleasure and avoid pain. In fact, it has been said that the desire to find pleasure and avoid pain is behind every other motivation. Some say that pleasure and pain are really the only two motivators in life.

We know pain can motivate people to change. And we know that the promise of pleasure has motivated people to do all kinds of things that may or may not have been in their interest. We know that some people are drawn towards pleasure like moths towards a flame. And some people find pleasure in pain, either their own pain or the pain of others.

Stack the motivational deck in your favor

Is it possible to have more than one motivation at a

time? Yes. In fact, the more motivations a person has, the more motivated that person will be. I call the layering of motivations 'stacking.' Layered motivations stack the deck in favor of initiative. With a big enough stack, motivation is practically unstoppable.

The value of recognizing these motivations in yourself is that you can stack the deck of your motivations and get yourself to do and follow through on almost anything.

For example: Writing a book is a big endeavor. It takes tremendous amounts of time, energy and focus. To get it done, I give up a lot of quality time with my family, relaxation time, and time to work on other projects. But I am motivated to write this book because I believe that getting this information to as many people as possible is the right thing to do. That's one layer. If I also fear that our society is heading in the wrong direction because people don't know how to protect themselves from negative persuasion agendas, that's another layer, and my resolve is strengthened to work quickly. And as I consider taking on the project, it occurs to me that the book can be a source of passive income for my family, maybe even a rich reward for a successful result. The stack gets taller, and my resolve grows stronger. And I must admit that I derive a great deal of esteem from completing books. Now my motivational stack is an even more powerful base for my efforts.

Now I believe that the purpose of my life, the reason I've been given the ability to speak and write, is to do what I can to make the world a better place for the children of the world, and for my family and friends right now. I put that into the stack. I find great pleasure in the creative process of crafting a book. Into the stack it goes. My stack has many layers. My motivation is strong. I am a force of nature. I am driven to research, learn, write, develop, test, and ultimately succeed. The fact that you are reading this book is proof of the power of my motivational stack. What's in your stack?

Find out why

The value of recognizing these motivations in others is that they can serve as powerful guides about what to say when you want to be persuasive. And these motivations are not hard to recognize. Simply find your own motivation for doing what you do, and suddenly you recognize motivation in others.

Just how can you find out the motivation of yourself or anyone else? Sometimes it is obvious. Just knowing it is there, you can look and listen for it. People tell you their motivations much of the time. But when the time is right for you to find out why someone thinks and feels the way they do, why someone might be persuaded to adopt your proposition, then that's the time to ask why questions.

Why questions become most valuable once you know who, what, where, when and how, because they help you to understand motivation, and motivation is part of the MAP. Finding the MAP gives you the key information you need to be persuasive.

Ask the following questions to learn your TOWARD motivations, or the TOWARD motivations of someone else.

What do you like about _____?
Why do you like it?
Why is that important to you?

Ask the following questions to learn your AWAY motivations or the AWAY motivations of someone else.

What don't you like about _____?
Why don't you like it?
Why is that important to you (or NOT important to you)?

In the next two chapters, we'll explore two other powerful pieces in the MAP of personal reality, Access Language and Position. When you're ready to continue the search, meet me in the next chapter.

10

FIND THE MAP: ACCESS LANGUAGE

We're studying our mission of finding the MAP. First, we found motivation. The second thing we find is that the second letter in the acronym MAP is an A. The A stands for Access Language, which is the language that expresses a person's preferred sense system for making sense. If that makes no sense to you, stick with me, keep your eyes and ears open, and give me a chance to explain.

I think you will agree that all people have at least five agreed-upon-senses, sight, sound, smell, taste and feeling. Most people have at least one system that they are more practiced at paying attention to than the others. Some people are more aware of what they see (sight,) others what they hear (sound,) and yet others what they feel (feeling.) This accounts for differences in learning styles. Some people read books, and can see what someone is saying with their words. Others listen to audio books, because it helps to hear someone say the words. And yet others need to engage in an activity in order to understand how to do something. So there are different ways of making sense. And each person makes different use of the same 5 senses.

I'm delighted to show you, tell you about, and hand you this powerful communication tool. First, here are a few examples of access language to illustrate, explain and demonstrate just what access language means.

I was holding a conversation with the head of an association interested in hiring me as a speaker for an upcoming event. She told me that it was HARD TO GET A HANDLE on TACKLING the problems the organization faced. Later, when describing my proposed program, I told her that I had a feeling my program would help people better grasp the problems, and smooth the way for solid solutions that were within their reach. Because I used lots of feeling words, I was able to put her mind (and body) at ease.

One of my private practice clients is an artist. One day, we were looking at his art, and his eyes grew dark as he said: "I see where I can be a better husband and father. But when I look at all the opportunities I've missed, it is clear to me that I was showing off instead of showing my kids a better way, that I have muddied the situation with my wife and acted like a dimwit when I should have been seeing her good intentions and helping her see mine." I showed him another way of looking at this. "No need to be so blue. Starting today, things are looking up! You've got a vivid imagination. Now that you're shining a bright light on your behavior, can you see a way clear to a new start?" Because I used the language of sight, I was more easily able to help him see a way forward.

I was talking with one of my students. She was explaining to me that she stopped trying to talk to her mom about her challenges in life. She said that her mom just can't hear what she's saying, that she interrupts and starts blabbing and blabbering on, speaking negatively about other people, talking at her instead of with her, and that her words are so hurtful sometimes that when she gets off the phone, her ears are ringing. I said, "That sounds awful! I hear that talking with your mom creates a lot of disharmony in your life." My student replied, "It sure does." "What if there was a way for you to get past the noise and clear up the relationship?" "I'm all ears," she replied. Because I used the language of sound, she could hear where I was coming from, and I could advise her on ways to improve the relationship.

When people describe their experience, whether by talking, or in writing, they must make use of their senses to do so, since our sense systems are a primary means for interacting with the world. Access language tells an astute persuader how a person prefers to pay attention through his or her sense systems. Consider the language of sight. It is the language of light and dark, of color and hue, of shape and appearance. Do you see what I'm saying? The language of sound speaks of volume, tone, pitch and timbre. Does that ring true for you? The language of feeling speaks of sensation and emotion. Can you grasp the implications of this? The language of taste and smell are closely linked to each other, because such is the arrangement of the human nervous system that smell is a key component of taste. Smell is particularly evocative, in that it easily triggers our earliest memories. And using access language will give you that sweet smell of success, or at least a taste of the possibilities!

Our sensory preferences determine the access language that we use. A person with a visual preference is likely to use visual words. A person with an auditory preference is likely to use words that refer to sound. A person who prefers feelings is likely to speak with the words of sensation and emotion. Some people, however, speak more objectively or in the abstract. You can recognize when this is happening. It requires more of an effort on your part to pay attention to it, because it literally doesn't make sense.

Sensory language is more powerful at engaging others than abstract language. When you season your words with pictures, sounds and feelings, you trigger the senses of your listeners, and free them from the effort required to make sense where no sense is being made. But for now, I want you to begin to notice the preferences of the people around you for making sense of the world. Just like any other form of blending, you can use the preferred access language of a person to build trust and increase interest in what you have to say.

The simplest way to use access language is by learning to use a few key phrases as seasoning, when responding to a person to whom you are listening.

Sight:

I see what you mean. That looks possible. Can you shed a little more light on that for me? It's beginning to dawn on me! Don't keep me in the dark any longer! Sorry, my memory is a little cloudy today. I see a whole spectrum of possibilities. That's a shining example. What a bright idea!

Sound:

That's music to my ears. Your words ring true. All that jazz. I hear you, loud and clear. We can orchestrate this campaign. A little tune up and we're ready. We work together in perfect harmony. You are clearing up the static. Thanks for helping me get past the noise.

Feeling:

Can you handle this? Not too tough? A soft touch. I can't quite put my finger on it. I've got to hand it to you. I feel like success is within our reach. I don't want to put this

71

on you. Together we can do the heavy lifting. It's hard to push ahead, but we can smooth the way. Iron out the wrinkles. We'll begin the drumbeat, and soon everyone will jump on board.

Smell and Taste:

Your palette can distinguish between four basic tastes: Salty, bitter, sweet and sour. And each of these can be used to convey different feelings. Tasty. Scrumptious. That's really sweet of you. Let's not end this on a sour note. We don't want to stay until the bitter end.   Last one in is a rotten egg. Whatever we do, it should be in the best possible taste.   Give it to me in plain vanilla. Too bland? What a delicious idea! That's good food for thought. Let me chew on this for a while. I'd like time to digest what was said. That went down well.

Unspecified language consists of words and phrases that you are likely to find in the verbal expressions of the cerebral and objectively trained - such as educators and scientists.   Let's be cautious. I'm confident we can develop this. I'm determined to persevere.   I remain hopeful we can resolve this.   I'm optimistic! I'm puzzled. I'm relieved. That is very thoughtful. It has yet to be decided.

Now that you've had a taste of the language of the senses, the Access Language found in a person's MAP, it's time to help you get a handle on this in a useful way, to get you tuned up and dialed in, to show you more of the presence and possibility contained in the words people use to describe their experience, to assist you in the tasteful use of language so your efforts won't stink. Take a day to play with words. Then you'll be ready to assume the position in the next chapter!

New free Ship

Life By Design Ch 12
p135-143

Insulars   21-25
          34-40
          47-54

11

FIND THE MAP: POSITION

A position is a belief stated as a fact. We have them, we believe them, and we defend them. Most people assume the position easily. And once we assume a position, we tend to stick with it as long as possible. Positions are how we anchor our understanding of the world around us. Once we fix our positions, we defend them like castles; building logical fortifications and emotional moats behind which we can shoot down any assailants who dare to challenge us.

When two people or parties take positions and defend them, a long battle of attrition ensues, each person attacking the other's position, trying to undermine it or outright destroy it. At best, the victor wins a hollow victory, as the beaten and vanquished opponent is coerced into submission and surrender. This is clearly not a good environment for persuasion. And this is specifically why I say that if you need to be right, you're doing it wrong.

Taking a position about someone's position is clearly not the solution. The real solution to dealing with positions

73

is to introduce doubt, reframe meaning, or find out the interests behind positions and address those interests in new and creative ways. Persuasion happens when positions change.

Strong Position, Weak Position, Opposition

Positions, like drugs and alcohol, come in different strengths, strong, weak and opposition. Strong positions are tied to a person's sense of identity, and are buttressed with conviction. A person with a strong position has likely defined it in stark terms, black and white, no shades of grey. A person with a strong position will not easily change their mind. The typical effect of a strong position is to polarize the positions of people around it (you're either with me or against me), and the likely reaction to a strong position is to defend one's own position against it.

There has to be a better way of dealing with strong positions, and there is. The more rigid the position, the more susceptible it is to small changes. Small changes in meaning can have huge side effects. Like in a game of Jenga, if you pull out the smallest piece at the base the whole tower might come crashing down. When a position falls, everything related to it tends to fall with it, and this can happen really fast. Use caution when undermining strong positions, as people tend to quickly become confused and angry about what was lost. A better choice is to help preserve a strong position, ask questions to introduce uncertainty about an aspect it, and then reframe the meaning of that aspect. This avoids the anger and confusion of a crumbling position, and helps people protect their sense of identity.

Weak positions, on the other hand, are surrounded by doubts. Succeed in understanding the doubts and a person will quickly accept an alternative idea that addresses those doubts. The person with a weak position is probably not fully convinced of it himself, and was already keeping his options open before you showed up with your proposition.

74

There is a third kind of position, called Opposition. It is the position opposite to your own. When dealing with opposition, it is your position that is in play. Some people may oppose your idea because they believe it goes against or undermines something they value, and is therefore wrong. If you acknowledge their concern, then reveal to them how their opposition undermines the same value (in the form of a question that requires an answer from them) they may have to make an adjustment.

Some people may oppose your idea because they believe it is unnecessary, wasteful and unrewarding. If you acknowledge the importance of not doing what is unnecessary, wasteful and unrewarding, then reveal how a failure to act on your idea will be wasteful, unnecessary and unrewarding (in the form of a question that requires an answer from them) they may have to make an adjustment.

Some people may oppose your idea because they believe it is destined to fail. Acknowledge this possibility, then reveal how a failure to act is a guarantee of failure (in the form of a question that requires an answer from them) and they may have to make an adjustment.

Some people will oppose your idea because they have unanswered questions. (Is it necessary? How will it be implemented?) Acknowledge and answer their questions, and their opposition will evaporate.

Some people are opposed to an idea because they feel they've been left out of the process. Draw them in, give them a role, and their opposition evaporates.

And some will oppose your idea because of a personal dislike or distrust of the people who favor it. Acknowledge this, and then provide evidence of people they like or trust who also favor it (in the form of a question that requires them to answer), and they will make an adjustment.

75

In each case, understanding the motivations behind opposition will give you the information you need in order to speak persuasively and address the concerns.

The Polarity Response

Opposition draws its strength from standing against another position. So it is possible to create opposition in others by voicing your own strong positions before understanding theirs. Yet some opposition is simply created out of thin air by people who oppose as a way of standing out from the crowd. A person opposed for opposition's sake is a contrarian, and his behavior is called a Polarity Response. For him, opposition is a way to assert his identity, and give him self a sense of independence, importance and control.   A contrarian is likely to resist any obvious attempt at persuasion, which means that subtlety how you win the day.

The key to dealing with a contrarian is first to notice that it is happening, and then play the polarity of it.   You can notice it is happening because the position is completely and unequivocally against your position. For example, the contrarian declares that your idea "won't work, never did, never will, no way."   To play the polarity, first you agree with his position about your position. "You're right. It won't work. No way, no how." This makes it a very uncomfortable and confusing situation for him. How can he disagree with you if you agree with him? Then you go one step further and make the failure of the idea his responsibility. "Not even you could find a way to make it work!" This virtually guarantees that a contrarian will respond, "Oh yeah? Well, you're wrong. Here's how to make it work!" If the contrarian says, "You don't know what you're talking about," you reply, "You're right. I don't know what I'm talking about, and you do." Then you pause, to let the discomfort sink in. "So that means it is up to you to explain what I'm talking about." Don't be surprised if a contrarian abandons his position opposite to your own, thus removing himself as an obstacle from your way.

For the moment, suffice it to say (or don't, it is entirely up to you!) that whenever you face opposition, it is useful to know as much about it as possible.

To summarize: People assume the position when they mistake their belief for the truth. Positions come in different strengths, from strong, to weak, to opposition. What can you do with positions? You can sow seeds of doubt with questions. You can reframe the meaning of some small aspect of a position, while retaining the position. And as you gain insight and understanding into the reasons and interests behind a position, you can take this information into account when presenting your proposition.

In the next chapter, we'll explore the nine information gates inside of every position, and how to ask questions about a position that take you through those gates to the deeper connections that hold it together. Information gate questions sometimes make connections fall apart, and open a larger gate to new opportunity. Want to find out more? Meet me in the next chapter.

12

INFORMATION GATES

In a previous chapter, we explored a simple listening strategy for going deeper into the deep structure behind the surface of a person's communication. But what if there was a way to go REALLY deep? What if there was a way to know a person's motivation for change? What if you could identify gaps in a person's position big enough for new information to get through? Would that be useful to you? Indeed, such are the skills of master people-helpers, persuaders and change artists. Read on if you want to learn a second way of listening, and gain access to the questions that open up the information gates hidden in the everyday words people use to describe their experience.

In the English language, there are 9 information gates that separate surface structure from the deeper structure of meaning. These gates are verbal expressions of limitations in the people represent their own experiences to themselves. It isn't difficult to get to the information on the other side of those gates. You just have to recognize the gates, so that you can unlock them with questions. Once unlocked, you can go ever deeper into the mindset of your persuadee, and open up new possibilities. This also gives you several choices about how to proceed once through the gate. You could ask for a counter-example (an example of how what the person said is not true). You could offer a counter-example and ask for a response. Or you could transition with a summary and a closed-ended question, and then use what you've learned to present your persuasion proposition. But it is driving through the gate that makes these options possible.

The best way I know for you to learn these information-tion gates and the questions that open them is with a little something I call 'Driving The Taxi.' Burt Miller, New York City taxi driver, told me that there are a few essential ingre-dients for driving a taxicab successfully. You need a comprehensive understanding of how your city is laid out. You need an excellent reference map, committed to memory when possible. And you need to know what questions to ask and when to ask them to get your fare to their destination.

One midsummer's night, Burt was sitting in his cab outside of a disco. A lady came out, got in the back seat of his cab, and then began sobbing uncontrollably. "Hey, lady, you alright? What's going on?" Burt asked. Her reply, a repeatedly muttered "Nobody cares about me. Nobody loves me." She chanted these words over and over again. Burt said, "Lady, who doesn't love you?" She stopped crying for a moment, looked confusedly at Burt, then blurted out the name "Tom" as she started sobbing again.

Burt told me that such is the power of questions. In a single question, he was able to reduce 6 and a half billion people (nobody) to one person (Tom.) Burt told me that if somebody says "Take me to the river," he wants to know "Which river specifically? We got two of 'em!" When somebody says, "Follow that car," Burt has the good sense to ask, "Hey pal, which car? We're surrounded by 'em!" Burt taught me that to drive a cab, there's nothing as important as asking questions that get you specific answers.

The surface structure of a sentence is inevitably a generalization that leaves out much specific information. So every sentence presents a variety of possible gates to drive through. You get to choose your gate, and your decision determines where you get to on the other side. If you pick a gate that yields little in the way of useful information, you can always back up and try another one. However, a warning is in order here. The questions presented in this chapter can also cause the gates to slam shut and stay closed forever! That is what will happen if you fail to blend while asking the questions.

Blending is essential when asking questions that go into the deeper structure of a person's personal reality. In addition to blending with body posture and facial expressions and the like, you also can blend with a person's pace and timing. Fast pace, speed up. Slow pace, slow down. You can also notice whether a person is talking about the past, the present or the future, and adjust your questions accordingly.

Just remember that without blending, the questions you are about to learn could lead a person to feel as if they were being interrogated! Take your time when asking these questions, and always backtrack before asking a question. You don't have to ask all the questions at once. You can pause between answers, too. One at a time, taking your time, is a smarter and healthier approach. With that firmly in mind, here are the gates and the questions that take you from surface to deep, from limitation to possibility.

Gate 1: CONFUSION - Missing "W"

When people are confused, it's usually because they are missing a few W's. The fact is, if you ask people how questions long enough without occasionally referencing the what, who, where and when, people tend to go into a trance state, and use confusion as a substitute for what they do not know. That's ok, because confusion is a gateway to new understanding. But someone has to go through that gate. With the right question, that can be you.

The missing "W" refers to people (who), places (where), things (what), and time (when.) When people express a limiting idea, like "nobody cares" you can ask, "Who doesn't care specifically?" or "Nobody cares about what?" or "Where don't they care?" or even "When don't they care?" If someone tells you that, "I lost my way," you can ask "Where did you lose it specifically?" or "What way did you lose?" or "When did you lose your way?" If someone says, "I don't have enough," you can ask "What don't you have enough of specifically?" If someone says, "I don't have time," you can ask "When don't you have time specifically?" Or "Time for what, specifically?" It is usually a good idea to find out the nouns of who, what, where and when, before driving through other gates. A misunderstanding of something so basic can send you down a detour from which it is difficult to return. Ask for nouns before verbs.

Gate 2: INACTION – Missing Process

When people don't move forward, it could be because they don't know how. They may know what, who, where and when, even why, but without knowing how to proceed, the only action is inaction. So they stop, and wait for the gate to open. You can open this gate with the right question, and find the deeper structure that leads to action!

All verbs are vague. They have to be. It just isn't possible to include all the information about how something happened each time a person describes what happened. If someone says, "You tricked me!" you can ask "How did I trick you?" If someone tells you "You're not listening to me!" you can ask, "How am I not listening to you?" or even "How do you know I'm not listening to you?" By gathering the deeper structure of the statement, you find out that certain of your behaviors influenced the person to feel tricked or to believe they weren't being heard. Thanks to the additional information you got by asking questions, you can know exactly what not to do or what you need to do in order to avoid the outcome in the future.

Here's a more complex example. If someone says, "I've already made up my mind," you can first ask "You've made up your mind about what, specifically?" followed by a "How, specifically, did you make up your mind?" She replies, "I examined the facts, and consulted with my advisors, and came to the conclusion that it isn't feasible." You backtrack, and then ask, "What facts did you examine?" or, "Which advisors did you consult with?" and then, "How did you come to that conclusion based on those facts?" or, "How did you decide to use those facts in drawing your conclusion?" Notice that you are not contradicting the person, simply gathering deep structure information. The person replies "It seemed obvious to me that it wouldn't work." You ask "Obvious in what way?" or "It wouldn't work in what way?" Each answer gives you more information. And interestingly, it gives the person more information about the inner workings of their own thought process.

At some point, you can then introduce new information, using a similar form or process as her own. "I'm wondering, what were the facts that you didn't consider? For example, what did you think about...." and provide a new fact in the form of a question.

Gate 3: STUCK – Verbs frozen into nouns

When people feel stuck, it could be that they have frozen their concept of where they are and what is going on. Bucky Fuller used to describe himself with the phrase, "I

82

think I am a verb." He recognized himself as a process, an unfolding reality of becoming. The Lord God in the Hebrew Bible uses a similar description, "I will become what I will become," often misquoted as "I am what I am" words that do not actually exist in the Hebrew language!) There is power in becoming. But many people think they are nouns. They think they are their names, their past, their image, and this puts definite limits on their imagination that lead to getting stuck, unable to move or change or develop. But with the right question, you can open this gate, and drive through to new possibilities.

A noun is a person, place or thing. A noun is tangible. A verb is a process word, and describes an action. Verbs don't, by nature, fit into wheelbarrows, but many nouns do. Yet when people limit themselves, they often do so by turning actions (verbs) into things (nouns). Can you hear a frozen verb in the word 'insults,' or 'frustration,' or 'failure?' Because insults is a frozen form of the action 'to insult.' Frustration is a frozen form of the action 'to frustrate.' Failure is a frozen form of the action 'to fail.' The word 'anger,' is a frozen form of the action 'to be angry.' Freezers allow us to objectify what we experience and create distance between undesired states and us. The problem is that it is next to impossible to change a desired state while it is in a frozen condition.

The way you thaw out a freezer is by asking a question that contains the verb form of the frozen word. "How did she insult you?" "What frustrated you?" "How did you fail?" "What angered you?"

A good way to learn about freezers is to practice making them! Freeze some verbs into nouns, and then thaw them out again. For example: Action becomes act. Discuss becomes discussion. Pay becomes payment. Once you can turn a verb into a noun and a noun into a verb, you will easily recognize the form of it, and know how to respond.

Here are a couple more examples:

Freezer: It was not my decision.
Question: How did you decide it?
Freezer: Consideration of this would be appreciated.
Question: What do you want me to consider?

Gate 4: INHIBITION – Limitation M.O.

When people believe in their limitations, they inhibit their creativity and replace it with reactivity. They wait by this gate, because they believe it to be locked. And they believe it to be locked for some 'very good reason.' Ask the right question, and you may find that possibility is waiting for you in the deeper structure of their personal reality.

You hear the term M.O. commonly used in police novels and movies. "That's his M.O.," says the hardnosed detective about the serial criminal. "He steals the wallet from the lady's purse and leaves a playing card in its place." For our purposes, M.O. refers to one of two modes of operation. Limitation and Possibility. In the art of persuasion, context specific modes of operation are what concern us, in that a person expressing limitation invites our interest in going deeper. The Limitation M.O. involves the use of words like 'can't,' 'should' or 'shouldn't,' 'must or mustn't,' and 'have to.' These words imply that there is no choice. Yet thinking it through, you can readily recognize that limitation itself is often a choice.

When a person says she can't do something, you can ask 'What would happen if you did?' in order to learn about the perceived danger in taking an action, or 'What stops you?' to find out more about the perceived obstacle standing in her way. And you don't have to stop there. You can follow through with other information gate questions, like missing 'W's, and vague verbs. When a person tells you that she should do something, you can ask 'What would happen if you don't?' to find out more about where the pressure to act is coming from. When a person tells you that she has to do something, you can ask 'What would happen if you didn't do it?' In this way, you can learn about perceived threats, pressures and obstacles.

Gate 5: ABSTRACTION – All or None

The tangible aspect of life, like goals and plans, formulas and strategies, processes and results, is specific in nature. But some people make a habit of expanding out from the specific to the general. That's a great way to get the big picture. But if a person expands all the way out, then everybody becomes a blur, nothing happens, and nobody can do anything about it. Ask the right question, and the specifics come clearly into view. Then everybody can do anything to change nothing into something in particular.

Universal words describe some aspect of the universe as if it is all or none. Yet your experience in life tells you that life is not binary, that nothing is forever, and everything and everybody has a moment. Odds are that when a person uses words like everybody, nobody, always, everything, never, anybody, etc., she is generalizing! And a universal generalization is an easy gate to drive through. All you have to do is ask for the specific example of the generalization. When you hear 'everybody,' or 'nobody,' you can ask 'who specifically?' When you hear always or never, you can ask "When specifically?" If someone tells you that there is 'never any time,' you can ask, "When isn't there time specifically?" And so on. Once you've gone from the generalization to the specific, it's easy to take the next step into the deep structure by finding another gate. "Lady, how do you know Tom doesn't love you?" and then "Tom doesn't love you in what way?"

Of course, sometimes people become very attached to their universals. In that case, you can exaggerate to reveal the impossibility of what they are saying. She tells you that 'Nobody cares!' and you say "Nobody? Really? Not one single person ever ever cares, not even one time?" Chances are she will come up with a counter-example. When she tells you that "Everybody knows that's how it's done," you can reply, 'Everybody knows? Every single person in the universe knows that's how it is always done every single time? There isn't maybe one person who doesn't know that?" However, be warned. When you exaggerate, make sure that your non-verbal behavior is sending messages that you're on their side, and simply exploring the fringes of their universe with simple questions. Doing this with some degree of subtlety is recommended. If she gets the impression that you are mocking or disapproving of her, there goes all the trust, and any hope of effecting change. All the trust? Well, maybe not all!

I recall a seminar that I gave in Texas back in the eighties, when the oil economy was in bad shape. I was doing my Difficult People and The Art of Communication program, and had just finished talking about dealing with Yes People. I called on a lady sitting towards the back of the room. She stood up and challenged me. "That won't work!" she declared, with all the certainty of a world-class expert. "What won't work?" I inquired innocently?" "None of it!" said she. "None of what?" I asked, more than a little intrigued. "None of what you're telling these naïve people." Ok, I thought to myself, try a different approach. "Ma'am, how do you know it won't work?" She was quick in her reply. "It's obvious." I had to ask, "Obvious to whom?" She came back with "Obvious to any thinking person." At that point, I guess I was feeling a little defensive. "Well, it's not obvious to me!" I said tentatively. "Then what's that say about you!" she harrumphed triumphantly. I tried challenging the universal with a bit of exaggeration, but she was really attached to it. "Ma'am, this won't work? Not at all?

Not even a little? Not maybe once in a while? Not for some people some of the time?" She was ready. "No."

I suppose this could have ended badly. But I got flexible. I played the polarity. "Well, then, I guess you're right. It won't work." I paused. "Not for you, no way, no how, not now." But then I left her an opening, and played for time. I said "I have no idea what led you to this conclusion, and I am interested. Please come talk with me at the end of the seminar. And I continued on as if she was with me. At the end of the day, she approached me, and apologized. She told me about a difficult office relationship, and admitted that she had become cynical as a result. Then she asked for my suggestions on what she might do differently! I suppose that, once she'd had time to think about it, her universal didn't even make sense to her. My question had opened up some room in her mind, and that made room for change.

Gate 6: BLAME – Cause and Effect

There are times when it seems that people are mere victims of circumstance, rather than authors and creators of their own experience. The formula of being the effect of a cause is as old as time, and is in common use whenever people are miserable. The right question can break the connection of cause to effect, and the spectacular effect is to find the deep structure information that seeks to be the cause of an effect.

The gist of cause-effect statements is that X somehow causes Y. It's a common linguistic behavior to attribute cause to an outside agent, particularly as a way of disclaiming ownership over an unsavory result. 'He made me miss the turn.' 'She made me forget what I was saying.' 'He wouldn't let me finish.' While sounding like a victim of circumstance may sound plausible, the fact is that it is rarely true. More often than not, we are victims of our own choices, perceptions, and assumptions. So when someone insists that an outside agency is forcing him to move in a particular direction or have a particular reaction, you can tease it apart by asking about the connection. How does X cause Y specifically?

'You make me mad' might sound plausible. But that's the time to become curious about "How, specifically, do I make you mad?" The response that you get when asking for the linkage between X and Y constitutes a person's internal linkage for 'makes me mad.' "You make me mad by ignoring me when I talk to you." She thinks you are ignoring her when she talks, and that thought makes her mad. You ask, innocently enough, about the process word, the verb 'ignore,' by asking the question "In what way do I ignore you?" She responds "By reading the paper when I talk." You ask, "So if I read the paper when you talk, that means I'm ignoring you?" "Yes," comes the response.

You now have a choice. If you choose, you can put the paper down, since you know what it means to her, and that will be the end of it. Or you can go deeper into her initial communication. "What would you rather I do when you talk to me?" "I want you to be interested." "Interested in what way?" "In what I'm saying!" "How would you know that I was interested in what you were saying?" "Well, you could nod your head when I talk, maybe ask me some questions." Now you know what to do while reading the paper so that she doesn't feel like she's being ignored. Nod your head, and ask questions.

But you have other choices, too. You can ask for a counter-example. "Do you ever read while someone's talking? Like reading a menu in a restaurant for example? Or a book on vacation?" "Yes, I suppose I have." "How is it possible for you to listen while reading?" 'Well,' comes the answer, 'sometimes I multitask.' 'Mmmhhhmmm,' you reply with understanding and a knowing look. Now you apply the new meaning to yourself, by asking a closed question that contains the new meaning and requires a yes in response. 'Is it possible that I can multitask too, and that when I'm holding a paper and you're talking, that I'm actually listening to you?' 'Yes, I suppose it's possible.' Now it's time to show a little gratitude for the new understanding. "Thank you. I'm glad you understand me better, because I certainly enjoy hearing what you have to say!' And now you can pick up the paper and finish reading that article in peace! It's your choice. You always have a choice. Nobody makes anybody do anything. Well, hardly anyone.

Gate 7: EXCUSES - Implied Cause and Effect

We all have our reasons. And any reason can be made to sound credible. But the inference and implication may not hold up in the presence of a simple question. When excuses fall apart, a gate opens, and persuasion becomes possible.

The Implied Cause statement is closely related to the Cause-Effect statement. In this case, a person implies a link between unrelated events. If X is true, then Y must follow. Or, if not for X, then Y would follow. For example, someone says 'I'd be in Toledo, but I lost my underwear.' Or 'I'd help you out, but I have things to do. ' Or 'I'd listen to you, but I'm up against a deadline.' Sure sounds feasible, doesn't it? Yet if you ask for the specific connection, quite often you'll find that the implied cause is just made up.

It reminds me of a story I heard years ago. A man went to his neighbor's farm and asked to borrow his rope. "Nope, can't do it," said the farmer. "What stops you from lending me your rope?" asked the neighbor. "I'm using it to tie up my milk," replied the farmer. Notice the implied cause pattern? If he wasn't tying up my milk, he could loan the guy his rope. The neighbor asked for the link. "Tie up your milk? For what purpose do you need to tie up your milk?" "I don't," said the farmer. "But when a man doesn't want to do something, one excuse is as good as another!" And that's how it is with Implied Cause statements.

Asking for the connection may open up some new possibilities, or at least expose the possibility that other choices exist. When a person says 'I'd do that for you, but I'm busy," you can say "Busy with what?" and then follow it up with, "How does being busy with that prevent you from doing this for me?" If a person says, "I'd be in Toledo but I lost my underwear," you can ask "How does losing your underwear prevent you from being in Toledo?" The answer may surprise you. Or disgust you. The important thing is that the linkage will no longer be implied. Either it will be explicit, as in "Because without my underwear, I'm uncomfortable traveling," or it will just fall apart. "I don't know."

I'd tell you about the next information gate, but I've got a lot on my mind. Reading that is your cue to wonder, "How does having a lot on your mind prevent you from telling me about the next information gate?" My answer: "It doesn't." Ok, here's the next information gate.

Gate 8: PROJECTION - Mind Reading

What people despise in others, they may be surprised to find in themselves. But sometimes, these qualities are too troubling to admit. It may seem easier to project them on others than deal with them in yourself. Ask the right questions, and you can create more honest reflections that lead away from rejection and towards a now open gate of change.

Any time a person claims to know the internal state of another person without asking or being told, there's a chance that they are mind reading. Not actually mind reading, of course. Just thinking they know what someone else is thinking. Like the lady at the psychic hotline who doesn't see the bankruptcy coming, people think they know a lot more about what's going in the world than they actually do. If you spend enough time observing people, I think you will agree with me on this: People are lousy mind readers! I'd go so far as to say that reading minds is hard, and changing minds is much easier. The fact is, most people don't even know much about what is on their own minds, much less what is on the mind of others!

When a person claims to know the internal state of another person, the question you ask is "How do you know?" Mind reading statements sound like "They don't care about me." "He has no respect for my authority." "You don't understand." "She never hears a word I say!" Such statements are ripe invitations for questions. When a person says, "They don't care about me," you can ask "How do you know they don't care about you?" The answer will provide information about a sensory cue and the meaning they make of it. "They don't even know I'm alive." You can ask, "How do you know that they don't even know you're alive?" "Because they don't smile at me when I come in." There's your sensory cue. No smile, they must not care.

When a person says, "You haven't heard a word I've said," you can reply, "How do you know I haven't heard a word you said?" The beauty of that last example is that you have demonstrated the opposite of their statement without contradicting them, just by asking a question that reveals that you have heard the words being said!

One of my consulting clients, Eliza, worked in a cubicle down the hall from the office of her manager Henry. Every day, she'd walk by his office, smile and say hello. "Hi, Henry." He'd sneer at her and, in a low and unpleasant voice, say "Hello Eliza." Then he'd turn away and focus on his work. Day after day, she tried to be friendly. Day after day, he'd respond in exactly the same way. Eventually Eliza gave up, deciding, "He doesn't like me." Once she made this decision, she looked for evidence and, of course, always found it. (That's the nature of sanity!) When she told me about having to work for Henry, and how hard it was to be in such a hostile environment, I became curious. I asked questions like 'hostile in what way,' and 'who is hostile,' and 'how do you know.' Then I asked for counter examples, other ways of accounting for Henry's behavior. By the end of our session, she admitted that she had no idea what he thought of her, or what his behavior meant. I taught her about the power of blending, and sent her on her way.

The next day, as she passed his cubicle, she gave it another try." "Hi, Henry," she said cheerfully. "Hello Eliza," came the gruff reply. She thought to herself, "I don't know why he's so nasty!" but then she caught herself. She was mind reading. She didn't know what his behavior meant. So she walked into his office, looked around, and saw a photograph of a horse on his desk. She pointed at it and said "Henry, is that your horse?" He looked up as if noticing her for the first time, and smiled. It was a weird smile, but a smile nonetheless. "Yes, that's my daughter's horse!" He got up, put his arm on her shoulder and guided her to a chair. "Let me tell you, my daughter has won more ribbons with that horse..." and he was off to the races, with so much to say that it shocked her. Funny thing, his voice was still gruff, low and unpleasant. It turns out that his voice just sounded that way. It didn't mean a thing.

Ok, I know what you're thinking. Actually, I don't. I just love the irony of saying that at this point. But it's a good guess that you could be wondering about the last information gate right about now. And here it is.

Gate 9: SUPERIORITY - Life Rulers

You need your own rules to play the game of life. Apply them to everybody else and you may be in for some serious disappointment. Looking down at others does little to build you up. People don't often succeed by climbing on a pedestal and demanding that the world should conform to their rules. They're more likely to succeed by learning the rules of the world and using them for leverage to make to-morrow better than today. The right questions help people step down from the pedestal, so they can go through the gate to find their own integrity.

We all have personal rules about our own behavior and choices. I think this is useful and valuable in our lives. For example, I have a personal rule about Thursday nights. My rule goes like this. ' I'm not available on Thursday nights, ever, for anything.' This rule works for me in a vari-ety of ways. I can put on my Superman colors and watch a science fiction movie. I can read a book or play my guitars. I can let my hair down, answer to no one, and be my own person. Why? Because Thursday night is my night. That's the rule.

But, what if I applied this rule to everyone else. What if I applied it to you? "No, you can't go out. It's Thursday night! Thursday nights are off limits!" Doesn't that seem a little heavy-handed? After all, who made me the boss of you? So living by your own rules is one thing. Requiring others to live by your personal rules is something else entirely. When a person applies their personal rule to somebody else's behavior, that's the information gate called 'Life Ruler.'

There's nothing wrong with having rules to govern your own life. Rules make it possible to win, to succeed, to overcome obstacles, to find fulfillment. Sometimes, just for fun, I try to imagine what the world would be like if people simply lived by their own rules, if their habits actually matched the values they profess, and their words matched their deeds; if parents set an example instead of making an example of their kids; if teachers demonstrated an interest in the material they teach instead of punishing students for their lack of interest; if politicians and religious leaders led by example instead of telling everyone else how to live. I can dream, but I'm not holding my breath. Because the world is filled with people and their personal rules, and a good deal of misery results from demanding and expecting others to obey them!

You have choices when people tell you their life rulers. The basic idea is to find out the source of the rule. If the person telling you the rule can own the rule, you've made progress. And if the rule comes from an unknown source, it may fall apart on its own. If someone tells you, in response to something you've said, "Nice people don't talk that way!" you can ask, "Where did you learn that nice people don't talk that way?" or 'According to whom?" If a person that never lets you get a word in edgewise (never?) or gets upset with you when you finally do get an edgewise word in, and tells you that "You shouldn't speak out of turn,' your natural curiosity can lead you to ask, "When specifically is my turn?" But you also have the option of asking for the source of that rule. "I shouldn't speak out of turn? According to whom? Where did you learn that?' At worst, the answer will be some kind of universal, as in "Everybody knows, that's how it's done." to which you can then reply, "Everybody knows? There is absolutely no other way by which it is done?"

You can have a lot of fun with this one, particularly in questioning undeserved authority, while at the same time opening up the possibility of something new happening in the deep structure of personal reality.

Using the 9 Gate Questions

Ok, it's time to hop in the taxi and play this all the way out, with a running example of a statement/question conversation that goes from surface to deep. Ready? Here we go. The situation: Dana is a regional manager for her company, and is responsible for multiple locations of their retail outlets. She wants one of her store managers, J.R., to use a different agency to hire contractors to do building maintenance, because her analysis reveals that J.R. is being overcharged for this service and is getting less than an adequate result. But Dana is new, and when she tells this to J.R, he balks.

Him: "I run this place, Dana. I have to do this my way. I'm sorry, but there's just no other choice."

Her: "What specifically do you have to do your way?"

Him: "I have to do the building maintenance my way."

Her: "I'm curious, what is your way of doing building maintenance?"

Him: "I hire the contractors, and then I let them make the decisions about costs."

Her: "So you hire the contractors and then let them make the cost decisions. That's interesting. You say you have to do this your way. Please help me understand. What would happen if you did it another way?"

Him: (defensively) "I'm responsible for this decision. If something goes wrong, it will be on me.

Her: "J.R., I appreciate your not wanting anything to go wrong. I don't either. Can you tell me something? Where do you hire your contractors?"

Him: "I use an online hiring system."

Her "Where did you learn about this online system?"

Him: "Everybody says they are the best."

Her: "Hmmm. Everybody? Really? Who says they are the best?"

Him: "Well, Moe told me about them. He uses them. He thinks they're the best in the business."

Her: "How do you know that Moe thinks they are the best in the business?"

Him: "He wouldn't have suggested them if they weren't the best."

Her: "How do you know he wouldn't have suggested them if they weren't the best?"

Him: "Well, why else would he suggest them?"

Her: "That's a good question. I wonder if you've ever been given bad driving directions from well intentioned people?"
Him: "I don't know what you mean."
Her: "Like when you're driving, and people are helpful, but don't really know what they're talking about."
Him: "Hmm. Yeah, ok, I get what you're saying.
Her: "What does Moe know about online hiring, anyway?"
Him: "I have no idea."
Her: "Is Moe familiar with any other agencies? For example, does he know about the Harris Agency?"
Him: "I really don't know if he does or not. I just assumed that he wouldn't have made the recommendation if it wasn't a good one."
Her: "I'm sure he meant well. Maybe you can do him a favor.
What do you think of this idea? Let's go talk with Moe and find out what he thinks about the service and prices at the Harris Agency?"
Him: "Um…that won't be necessary. This is my decision. I'll try your approach and we'll see how it works out. Thanks for bringing this to my attention."
Her: "Thanks for being flexible." I'll be back in a month. It's good to know that you personally have this situation under control."

Let's try another one, this time between a husband and a wife. He is taking a predictable argument and turning it into a persuasion opportunity.

Her: "You don't care about me anymore."
Him: "Oh. Huh. I don't care about you anymore. Really? I don't care about you anymore in what way specifically?
Her: "My feelings."
Him: "I don't care about your feelings? I'm sorry to hear that. Which feelings don't I care about?"

Her: "You never say anything nice, you never do anything nice, you never treat me nice.

Him: "Wow. Never? I never ever say or do anything nice, not one thing, not one time, ever, not even a little nice?"

Her: "Well, hardly ever. And when you do, it's only because you want something."

Him: "How do you know it's because I want something?

Her: "I can tell."

Him: "You can tell. Fair enough. How can you tell?"

Her: "You know. The way you look at me, it's obvious."

Him: "How do I look at you that tells you I want something from you?"

Her: "You get that look in your eye."

Him: "What is the look in my eye that tells you I want something from you?"

Her: "That mischievous look."

Him: "Is there ever a time when I have that look and don't want something from you?"

Her: "No."

Him: "Never? You can't think of a single time when I had that look and didn't want something from you?"

Her: "Well, I guess you look that way when you're trying to make me laugh, too."

Him: "When I try to make you laugh, is that what you mean by me wanting something from you?"

Her: "No." (She laughs)

Him: "How would you know if I didn't want something from you?"

Her: "I don't know. I guess I wouldn't know."

Him: "What if I told you when I did want something? That way, if I didn't tell you, you could assume I didn't want anything!"

Her: "I guess that seems reasonable."

Him: "That way I could be nice to you just because I care about you."

Her: "Yes, well, that would be nice."

Him: "Sweetheart, please notice what I'm about to say to you. There's nothing I want from you right now, but there is something I want for you. I want you to know without a doubt that I love you."

Her: "Aw, that's really sweet. Come here, I have a kiss I want to give you!"

Him: "If you insist, I aim to please!"

Health Implications in the 9 Gates

Since the early days of my private practice, I've worked with a number of patients confronting serious health problems. As a student of the mind/body connection, I've been fascinated with understanding how my patients organize their internal worlds and what connection, if any, there might be to the health problems they deal with. My useful assumption is that bad health is a position, that much of disease is frozen process, and that unfreezing the process and going deeper can yield great benefits for my patients. Using the information gate questions outlined in this chapter, I have been able to tease open perceived limitations in my patients' ideas about themselves and their world, reveal to them options they were previously unaware of, and in this way persuade them to recover their health. I can only tell you that something akin to miracles happen on occasion.

I attribute such changes to the fact that I am patient with my patients, that I show great interest in them, and I ask the questions that take them into their own deep structure. Once they go deep, they make new distinctions, find solutions, and sometimes initiate profound changes. As a result of this work, I have experienced firsthand the resourcefulness of human beings, no matter how limited they present themselves on the surface of their experience. If you have a health challenge, I invite you to investigate it in writing, using the information gate questions. Who knows? It couldn't hurt. It might help!

This was the longest chapter in the book so far. It contains some important keys that can make a real difference in your persuasive power. But knowing about them is one thing, being able to use them is something else entirely. To truly learn these information gates, I suggest that you practice making up 10 examples of each gate, along with the questions that would take you deeper. Next, write down one of your own limitations, and use the nine questions to open the gates and discover a deeper truth about yourself. Then, and only then, open the gate to the next chapter and meet me on the other side.

13

TRANSITIONAL OPENERS

Every persuasion interaction has three phases. Phase One is trust building and information gathering. Phase two is the transition, where you complete listening, and begin the shift to talking. And Phase three is when you present your persuasion proposition

But how do you know when you're done with Phase One and ready for Phase Two? You don't, so you have to guess.

Sometimes the end of a phase is dictated by time constraints, either yours or the person you seek to persuade. Sometimes, the end of a phase is a function of location, where you're in an elevator and your persuadee arrives at his or her floor and steps off, or you're in a busy corridor and you see people moving in your direction. And sometimes, in our best-case scenario, you arrive at the end of Phase One when you have learned enough about your persuadee to successfully make your presentation.

Transition: A Pivotal Moment

The transition phase is a pivotal moment on which everything that follows depends. Though it is the shortest phase of persuasion, it is deserving of your recognition and attention.

The purpose of a transitional phase is to summarize what you've learned, and prepare the way for what you are about to say. Your summary gives you an opportunity to accomplish three objectives. First, it gives you a way of assuring your persuadee that you have listened and understood. Second, it gives you a chance to highlight information that can increase acceptance of what you have to say. And third, the transition gives you a chance to 'tell them what you're going to tell them,' before you actually tell them.

A transition builds a bridge between what you've learned and what you have to say. To build this bridge, you need the starting pylons to rest in the territory of your persuadee's MAP. That's why the first part of a transition must establish a connection to what you've heard. Phrases like "Because of what you've told me," and "In light of what we've just discussed," and "Since (MAP info) is so important (to you, to us, to the team, for our project)" and "Based on what you've said," are easy beginnings for planting the pylons.

Next you tie the rope to the pylons, and place some boards beneath your feet to begin crossing over. This is the connective material of transitional openers, and there are a few ways to go about it.

Ask for Permission

"...May I tell you about a way that we can (short summary of the desired outcome)?" If you choose to ask for permission, make sure that you wait to receive it before proceeding. Because this is a question, it requires a response, thus involving your persuadee. Asking for permission tells people that they are involved in what they are about to hear because you value, recognize and appreciate them. Once someone gives you permission, his or her consent becomes the green light for you to present your persuasion proposition. Asking permission works, because anything you say with permission is bound to find a more receptive audience than anything you say without it.

This works well with almost everyone. Specifically, it works well with people who have the communication needs for approval and appreciation. You can vary the degree of directness, and understate it with care and consideration, or say it with enthusiasm, depending on what you've learned about your persuadee. Or ask for it with care and enthusiasm. But ask for it.

Permission also gives your persuadee something to say yes to, and yes is almost always a good beginning to persuasion. In fact, asking permission is so powerful that you can continue to ask permission throughout Phase Three/Presentation. "May I describe the benefits of my proposal?" "May I offer you a demonstration?" "May I give you a sample?" Permission is a powerful persuader, because it comes from your persuadee, and means you have their consent to hear what you have to say.

Here's a classic use of asking for permission, with a funny response. Someone says to you, "May I ask you a question?" And you reply, "You just did." They then say, "May I ask you another question right after this one?" I don't know why, but that always makes me laugh! (Thank you Mr. Data!)

But really, if you think it through, asking for permission to ask a question before asking the question is a wonderful way of getting someone to really think about their answer when your question comes their way. It's a heads-up that a response is desired, and it allows your persuadee to mentally get in position to answer whatever you are about to ask. It gets attention, and holds it.

Claim the bridge

"...I want to tell you about (Provide a short summary of your desired outcome.)"

This works well when time is short and there are other items on the agenda. It also works great with the communication need for action, because it is direct and to the point.

One Step At A Time

"...I want to discuss/explore/develop an idea with you that (Short summary of the desired outcome.)" This connective phrase offers opportunity for discussion, and the implication is that your proposition is a work in progress with a few details to iron out. This slightly indirect approach works well when submitting an idea to your team, or when you are dealing with someone with the communication need for accuracy. It leverages the fact that people are more likely to agree to an idea that they own.

If you notice that your persuadee isn't crossing the bridge with you at any point, stop, go back into Phase One and find the missing information, before re-entering Phase Two. You do not need to provide your proposal yet. The purpose of the Opener is to give you an interesting start. Combine the above with what follows and you'll have the ingredients for a smooth transition.

A Thought Provoking Statement:

What do people find thought provoking? A paradox or a challenge to the existing paradigm will quickly do the trick.

"If you don't care about your results, then don't give your attention to what I'm about to say."

"When the going gets tough, the tough get going."

"If there's one thing I know, it's that you can't take anything for granted."

Thought provoking statements are difficult to understand, at least when you first hear them. And that's why they make you think. This is a great thing to do with someone who you suspect is or might be disinterested in your proposal. The intent is to engage their mind before their mind disengages from you. Throw down the gauntlet with a thought provoking statement, and then follow that up with something substantial that they can get their mind around, and you will have created an opening for the art of persuasion.

You can also provoke thought with humor. There are literally hundreds of clever and thought provoking ideas circulating on the Internet these days. Chances are you've gotten a few in your email. Here are just a few examples that could be used to open

"The definition of insanity is doing the same thing over and over and expecting a different outcome. No wonder people sometimes act a little crazy around here!"

"If quitters never win, and winners never quit, then who came up with 'Quit while you're ahead?'"

"If work is so great, why do we pay people to do it?"

"If you try to fail and succeed, what have you done?"

Thought provoking questions aren't easy to answer. But they grease the wheels of thought. Please note: If you use this opener, the next thing you say should make a lot of sense! Your persuadee will be grateful for it, because it allows them a way out of the paradox and gives them a way to save face and look like they know exactly what you mean.

Ask for a YES

Closely related to asking for permission is asking for agreement! If you're certain that you'll get a yes of agreement to a particular idea, you can say it as a question as a way of transitioning into your presentation.

This happened to a friend just the other day. A credit card company called about suspicious activity on his card. It turned out that the activity was two reoccurring transactions. It was the third such incident in three months. My friend said, "You want me to carry your card, right?" And the fraud protection guy said, "Yes." "And you know that carrying your card requires me to have confidence that I can use it when I need it, right?" "Yes, sir, of course...' "And you understand that when you put a security hold on a credit card for no good reason, and a person is traveling and conducting business, it might cost them money and time and be bad for their business, right?" "Yes, of course." And there ended my friend's transition. He opened with, "Well I'm glad you understand, because I'd like you to find a way of protecting my card from fraud while preventing unnecessary holds on it." The result: They found a middle ground solution that works to protect both his interests as a consumer and the company's interest in preventing fraud.

'"Have you ever wondered why we don't get good ideas from our employees?" If you know the answer you're going to get back is yes, asking for a yes is a great place to open a persuasive proposition.

"How many of you can think of one person that you just can't stand?" That's how I start my live training and speeches on the subject of difficult people. And hands always go up. Why wouldn't they? People come to that program because they think somebody is driving them crazy! "Can you think of two people?" Quite a few hands still go up. "Three or more problem people in your life?" Hands keep going up! The problem of problem people has to be solved. If you had a problem with someone behaving badly, wouldn't you want to know how to solve it? I know how to solve it. Maybe that's why the book I coauthored on 'Dealing With People You Can't Stand' is an international bestseller. (Pardon my shameless plug!)

Sales professionals know the power of building a YES Set, something we'll explore in greater depth in the chapter on Closing. But the gist of it is that every time a person says yes, you create momentum for whatever you say next. And beginning your persuasion proposition with momentum is what openers are all about!

Short Story

"Let me tell you a story about someone just like you who overcame numerous obstacles and changed the world."

Stories involve people just like you and me having experiences from which we can learn their lessons. The power of narrative is such that story telling is one of humanity's best tricks for passing along wisdom, teaching important principles, and imparting essential knowledge. Stories give us a safe place to identify, to get caught up, and to safely reflect on our situation and ourselves. Stories work when they are about people, because it is natural for people to care about people. I'll have more to say on the use of narrative in the chapter on Persuasion Guides.

But that reminds me of a story.

"Life is like a bowl of chicken soup." So said the famous teacher as he lay dying in his bed. His students came from miles around, and they patiently formed a line, from the brightest of them at the front, to the dullest of them at the back, hoping to hear his final words before he was gone forever. The line stretched out of the teacher's house, around the block and down the street for a mile. Each time the teacher spoke, the students passed his words back through the line in response to the student behind each student asking, "What did he say?" And so, the new teaching, "Life is like a bowl of chicken soup," made its way to the end of the line, with each student nodding their head on hearing the words as if they completely understood. But when the words made their way to the last student in line, that student scratched his head, perplexed, mystified even, by this new teaching. Finally, he had to ask the student in front of him to explain.

"Life is like a bowl of chicken soup?" But the student in front of him couldn't tell him what it meant, so he in turn passed the question forward. Eventually, the question made it's way from the end of the line to the front of the line, where the brightest student leaned down and quietly asked the teacher the question. "Oh great teacher, help us to understand your teaching. How is life like a bowl of chicken soup?" The teacher contemplated the question for a very long time. Then, with great effort, he signaled to come closer and hear the response given with his last breath. "Ok," he shrugged, "life is NOT like a bowl of chicken soup!" And then he died.

Testimonials

Testimonials are short, personal stories that promote an idea, product or service. The upside of a testimonial is that it creates a reference point by which to evaluate a claim. The downside is that a testimonial can set a level of expectation that is hard to live up to!

Recently, a sales person tried to convince me to try out his new product. He gave me 5 testimonials, each one more powerful than the last, about how the product was the most amazing thing ever, how the product had changed someone's life, how the product had saved someone scores of money, how the product prevented a terrible problem, and so on. Initially, I was somewhat open to the idea. But with each hyperbolic testimonial, I found myself believing less and less, until I didn't believe anything the sales person had to say. Surely, if the product were as great as these people claimed, I would have heard such miracle stories from someone NOT selling the product!

The point? Better to tell me something is good, and back that up with a testimonial, than to tell me it is better than I can believe, and here are the testimonials to prove it. If you have testimony to share, that's great. But remember that if it sounds too good to be true, it probably is.

Don't get me wrong. I do not doubt that sometimes, amazing things happen in life. Maybe all those testimonials were true. But I know for a fact that people can have amazing experiences with almost anything, since the power of belief is such a strong force in our lives. And if what's being sold requires your persuadee's belief for it to work, then they, like me, may come to believe it doesn't work and won't work. It seems to me that there's a sucker born every minute, and a seeker too! That little aphorism makes a nice transition to our next opener.

Relevant Quote or Aphorism

"If you would persuade, you must appeal to interest rather than intellect."

So said Ben Franklin, and I think he got it exactly right. A quote is a saying that someone said, and you are saying it to highlight an important aspect of your proposition. The quote or aphorism you choose must be relevant to your topic, and have the power to grab attention. Quotes, and aphorisms, have the benefit of adding authority to your words. Whose authority? Whomever you are quoting. You only need provide attribution for your quote if you desire to grant its authority to yourself. You can even quote yourself! "As I often say, change your mind, change your life, change your world." And even an anonymous quote has the power to grant authority, if the quote is compelling enough, since the assumption made is that the person who said something so interesting was important enough to be quoted.

Hippocrates wrote that, "Life is short, art is long, opportunity fleeting, experimenting dangerous, reasoning difficult." He was the first to use the word aphorism, in a book aptly titled Aphorisms. An aphorism is a brief expression of an important principle that you seek to employ in your pitch. Aphorisms are best known for containing a lot of information in very few words, through the clever turn of a phrase, pun, or paradox. I've heard it said that an aphorism is more like a carry on bag than a suitcase. You can easily place it in the overhead compartment of your mind. Aphorisms often offer insight into the human condition, while sometimes offering a jaded view of whichever point they choose to prick.

You can transition with an aphorism, and then make sense out of it with your proposition.

"Time heals all wounds, and time wounds all heels. So yes, our competitor undercut us with our client base. But if we adapt to our changing environment, we can gain advantage while he will eventually squander any advantage he has gained."

"A committee is a dark alley down which ideas are led to be strangled. Let's try this instead."

Let's review: You can use a quote:

"H.G.Wells wrote that civilization is a race between catastrophe and education."

"According to Mark Twain, it ain't what you don't know that gets you into trouble. It's what you know for sure that just ain't so."

"Yogi Berra had a way of cutting right to the point, when he cautioned that 'You got to be careful if you don't know where you're going, because you might not get there."

Or you can use a familiar saying:

"There's no time like the present."

"Better to light a candle than curse the darkness."

"Even a stopped clock is right twice a day."

Or you can use one of my sayings (just give me some credit for it!).

"You know the saying, 'Think outside the box?' Well, Dr. Rick says 'Don't get in the box!'"

And that makes a nice transition for our next kind of transition.

Hopeful or Terrifying Comparison:

"We can change the world, or be changed by the world." Comparisons are great for making the complex simple (and the simple, complex!) We'll talk more about comparisons, how and why they work, in another chapter. But suffice it to say that when you make a comparison as an opener, you have the opportunity to highlight an important idea by comparing it to something important, or unimportant. But not just any comparison will do. For dramatic effect, you want to make a hopeful or terrifying comparison.

A hopeful comparison tells your persuadee that things can turn out better, as compared to how bad they are now, if they take your desired action. A terrifying comparison tells your persuadee that things may well turn out worse, compared to how bad or good they are now, unless they take your desired action. In both cases, you want to end the comparison with the point you seek to highlight. Otherwise, you leave your persuadee scratching their head, because not all comparisons are effective in creating change.

Historical Perspective:

"One year ago, our founder stood before us and challenged us to do better. Today, I'm happy (sad) to report that we have succeeded splendidly/we have failed miserably."

Once upon a time, journalists put their stories in perspective. They provided perspective and context for their stories, to help their readers have a better understanding of what they were reporting. Sadly, this practice has fallen out of use.

A few months ago, I read an article about a study that claims that taking anti-oxidant supplements appears to increase your chances of dying by 5%. The study appeared in the Journal of the American Medical Association, a prestigious medical journal that wears the mantle of authority of modern medicine. And the report appeared in just about every media outlet, from national TV news to my local paper. It is a well-known fact that more and more consumers are choosing to supplement their diet in the hopes of improving their health and avoiding the need to manage disease later in life with drugs and surgery. Something not mentioned in the article is that this might make supplements a direct competitor to drugs in the medical marketplace. The Journal derives significant revenue from drug advertising, and it derives no real income from health supplements advertising, I think it would have been interesting had the Journal or the media put this study in context. After all, a Center for Science in the Public Interest (CSPI) review of JAMA articles revealed that 11.3% of the articles reviewed had non-disclosed conflicts of interest.

And I found myself wondering, what are your chances of dying if you don't get enough anti-oxidants in your diet? Or for that matter, what is your percentage increase or decrease in chance of dying if you see a doctor instead of taking a supplement for your health problems? And just what is your percentage increase or decrease in chance of dying if you take more than one prescribed drug? But such questions weren't asked. And nowhere in the reporting of the anti-oxidant study, or in the study itself, was it mentioned that doctor-caused death is a leading cause of death in the United States. Nor was it mentioned that everything labeled has the potential to increase your chances of dying. Eating at home can kill you! Once we label it, we can prove it with a study. Eating out can kill you! Not eating can kill you! Taking a drug can kill you! Not taking a drug can kill you! Yikes! Does this mean that it's the studies that actually increase your odds of dying? No.

But a report that included some discussion of any of these things might have created a little context, some historical perspective through which the report could have been interpreted and made useful. In context, it seems unlikely that supplements are more likely to kill you than anything else. And other studies show the opposite of this study to be true. Alas, a little perspective was nowhere to be found.

When you use historical perspective as an opener, you provide context. You can use perspective as a way of showing the lineage of a problem, or highlighting progress, or demonstrating the adoption of a solution. In each case, history informs, edifies, and contextualizes important information for your persuadee. Use the format of 'then and now,' or 'Let's take a look back at what brought us to this moment in time,' or 'Let's look ahead at where we'll be if we make critical changes in our operation now." We'll be talking more about historical perspective shortly, when we explore organizing themes for your persuasion proposition.

What about statistics?

We'll discuss the role of statistics in persuasion later in the book. For now, the idea of a statistic as an opener is that it isn't enough to be on point, unless it either raises eyebrows or gets a good laugh. If it does neither, it's a boring opener that you'd be best not to use. The best statistics to use for openers are shocking!

"A recent survey of our employees reveals that 35% of them dread coming to work, 27% of them talk badly about us to their friends and family, and 68% feel indifferent and disinterested in what they do. Think about what that means for our organization for a moment."

Here's another one. "One out of every three people is an idiot. Look to your left. Now look to your right. If it isn't one of them, you're in trouble!"

Here's my personal favorite. "A recent study concludes that 83% of all statistics are made up." What? That's true! At least 90% of the time!

Now it's your turn

I recommend that you take some time developing several transitions and themes for your persuasion proposition. That's the best way I know to learn these, and the best way to be prepared to use them in Phase Two after you learn what you can in Phase One.

That's all I have to say on what to say when you transition from listening to talking. The rest of what you say has to do with your persuasion proposition, and my assumption is that you know more about that than I do! In the following chapters, I will provide you with some astonishingly powerful ideas about how to organize your proposition and what to emphasize in what you say for maximum impact and persuasion. So as soon as you're ready, read on and prepare to be astonished.

14

ORGANIZING THEMES

Perhaps the biggest difference between a written persuasion proposition and a spoken one is that, when it's
written down, your persuadee can look around, look forward,
go back, and basically keep track of where they are and
what's going on. When you talk to people, they have to be
able to follow you, while retaining some connection to what
you've already said. And since thinking is too energy-
expensive for many, your persuadee may get lost in what
you say unless you organize it in such a way as to help him
keep track.

That's where persuasion themes come in. If you organize your persuasion proposition around a theme, that
theme becomes the backbone that helps your persuadee track
of where you were, where you are, and where you're going.

There are many ways to organize information for
verbal delivery. I'm about to share with you ten of my personal favorites.

The Timeline

If you use historical perspective as your transition/opener, you may want to use the Timeline theme to organize your entire presentation. The timeline gives you a way to walk your persuadee from a moment in the past of your choosing, through the present moment, on into a future moment that results from your proposition, and watch, listen and learn as history unfolds. The formula is simple. "Here's how it was. Here's how it is. Here's how it can be, and will be if you agree to my proposal." A timeline theme allows you to draw connections between past and present, past and future, present and future, and everything in between. A timeline then helps you establish that there are consequences to previous actions and choices, and to potential actions and choices as well. A timeline allows you to create both context and momentum for change.

Problem & Solution

People have a natural mental tendency to frame life in terms of problems and solutions. The same is true in business. The problem & solution theme allows you to reveal the depth of a problem, the consequences of a problem, and tie your solution to the end of the problem. However, no matter how bad the problem or how unaware your persuadee is of the problem, you want the emphasis of what you say to be on the solution. Too much attention to problems and you run the risk of creating hopelessness rather than momentum for change.

Meeting The Challenge

Supposing that you have a situation where people feel so awful about a particular problem that some of them, maybe all of them, have given up hope of ever solving it. That happens after a prolonged period of a worsening situation. It also happens when people pay too close attention to a problem instead of paying attention to finding solutions. But no matter how it happens, when it happens, people despair. Under such conditions, talking about a problem and how to solve it is unlikely to be persuasive.

But do not despair! Find the challenge there! When you frame a problem as a challenge, your language naturally shifts to do or die, success or failure, rising or falling. Meeting a Challenge allows you to take an undeniably difficult situation based in fact and convert it to an emotionally powerful opportunity. This theme creates a license for empowered rhetoric.

Winston Churchill used this theme to harden the resolve of his countrymen for the bitter war ahead. John F. Kennedy, Robert Kennedy and Martin Luther King used this theme to engage the hearts and minds of people, young and old alike. Nelson Mandela used this theme to transform a divided country. Ronald Reagan used this theme to remind people of the power of possibility. Preachers use it. Teachers use it. The Mystery Men used it. And so can you.

You can wax poetic. "Let us boldly go into the fray, and always seek the better way. From coast to coast, from town to town, they shall not ever slow us down!"

You can use alliteration (beginning several words in sequence with the same sound.) "Each and every engineer has earned his place in this pantheon of possibility!"

You can give personality to objects and entities. "This antiquated phone system is threatening to bring our entire enterprise to a crawl. It wants to destroy us. It shall not succeed!"

You can use rhetorical questions. "Are we not proud of our service? Are we not capable of anything when we put our heads together? Have we not overcome seemingly insurmountable odds in the past? I say YES! What say you?"

You can repeat a key phrase to punctuate ideas. "We're number one! We're number one!"

Put them together, and your rhetoric can rally the recruits and ready their responsiveness! "We shall not go quietly into the night. We shall not give up without a fight. We will never give up. Never surrender. Victory will be ours!"

Of course, there's no need to go over the top. But the language of challenge, of success and failure, of victory and defeat, calls on the depth of people's feelings and the heights of their aspirations, on their hearts rather than just their minds, and allows you to create a rallying point that may indeed bring out the best in people and carry your proposition to fruition.

"It is true that we are faced with the challenge of preserving our environment for future generations while keeping our economy vital and growing. It is true that much depends on our meeting this challenge successfully. Yet we can meet this challenge head on. We can do the important things, the necessary things. We can be bigger than our excuses. We can demonstrate wisdom. We can make this plan our plan and go forward to our inevitable success."

Opportunity

I've heard it said that, in the Chinese language, the word CRISIS means 'Opportunity riding a dangerous wind.' So opportunity tends to come with risk attached. The greater the risk, the greater the potential gain.

The opportunity theme is perfect for a proposal targeted at the motivation for reward. You organize what you say to reveal what may be gained by adopting or implementing your idea, or what may be lost by the failure to seize the opportunity that has presented itself.

In every opportunity, there is leverage to make tomorrow better than yesterday. If your proposition can identify the point of maximum leverage, where doing the least will accomplish the most, you'll find it readily embraced. If, on the other hand, the leverage you identify is meager and the work required great, you may find that the opportunity theme is not ideal for your proposition. When control of congress shifts, it is because several candidates for office successfully use this theme. "This election represents your opportunity to put an end to the abuse of power that my opponent and his cronies have exercised, an opportunity to learn from the mistakes of the incumbent so that we can stop the bleeding and prevent such travesties in the future."

Features & Benefits

This is the classic sales pitch, and there's a reason for that. It's tried, it's true, and it works in some important ways. Features speak to the logical mind. They are based in fact, and describing them allows you tell your persuadee what your proposition is and how it works. Benefits appeal to emotion, by offering a feelings based set of reasons that explain why those features will make life better, the team stronger, the company healthier, the relationship more intimate. In other words, benefits tell people why they should care, what's in it for them to go along with you. Earlier in this book, we spent a good deal of time exploring motivations, and what you've learned can help guide you in deciding whether to emphasize features or benefits, or both. But when you have to choose, benefits speak more powerfully than features.

It is rare for a person to make a decision based on features, though it happens. Features matter, because sometimes people actually make practical decisions for practical reasons. If your idea, product or service offers features that address those reasons, the decision may be made accordingly. The dictates of science and engineering tend to require a focus, not on feelings, but on facts. And sometimes, a person is already of the general persuasion to support your proposition, and simply needs the hard details to come to a definitive moment of decision. You'll know this if you listened. In each of these cases, an emphasis on features would prove more beneficial than an emphasis on benefits.

However, most people make decisions based on emotion, and then justify their decisions using logic. (You'll learn more about this when we talk about the signal of Consistency, later on in the book.) So with most people, the benefits should get most of your verbal attention as you seek to maintain interest and win your persuadee's support. You present the features of your idea, product or service, and then connect those features to specific benefits that your persuadee will receive by making a favorable decision. The trick to successfully communicating benefits is to consider them from an effective viewpoint. Rather than describing benefits based on what appears beneficial to you, who knows the inside and out of the proposition, you want to take a beginner's mind. Recognize that your persuadee knows far less than you about your proposition, and consider what benefits they may find attractive in your proposition.

The Features and Benefits theme works best with products, and services. Yet it is possible to place the intangible realm of ideas and actions into this theme. You can describe the features and benefits of anything, including people and ideas. A person applying for a job can pitch their features

"I have a track record of promotion, impeccable integrity, and I've acquired the following skills acquired over time. I'm enthusiastic about my work, and I'm a creative thinker."

The key is to translate those features into benefits.

"What this means to you is that I am consistent and reliable, that my experience and knowledge will be readily available to serve the interests of this organization when the unexpected happens, and I will be a positive force and a source of high morale in the larger team and department. And it means I'm able to find new and better ways of doing things while cutting costs."

Make an Example

How do you take something that is complicated and not all that interesting, and make it into something personal to which your persuadee can relate? You put a human face on the details, by making a story out of it. Real or fictional, let your stories reveal the need for your proposal, or what can happen when your proposal is adopted. Let the people in your story show by their example and tell by their experience what you want your persuadee to know in making a decision.

Teaching by parable is a time honored method, and persuasive enough that some stories survive millennia. Yours only need last long enough to bring your persuadee to a moment of decision.

"I spoke with one of your constituents. He tells me that a conflict over water rights has left farmers stuck in the middle. Where they could be planting, their fields lie fallow. Where their children could be learning responsibility and service, they watch TV instead. He begged me to bring this to your attention, because he wants you to know this situation is intolerable. He gets it. Do you?"

People are interested in stories. And when you use a

story to illustrate your proposition, you not only have a way to gain and hold interest, you can use the story to lead to any point of your choosing.

Answer the Questions

When you have a high degree of certainty that your persuadee has a lot of questions about your proposal or recommendation, you can short circuit skepticism by asking and then answering those questions yourself. Or, you can ask for any questions and organize what you have to say around the interests those questions expressed. If the former, write them down where everyone can see them, or at least everyone can see you writing them down, then check them off as you answer them. If the latter, you can begin by asking and answering one question at a time, or asking several questions all at once.

"You may wonder, how will we change course, when all we've known to do is what we have done so far. How will we change our culture to be more helpful and friendly? Who will lead the charge? Who will keep the mission connected to the facts on the ground? These are important questions, and I intend to answer them."

Then answer each one in turn, summing up your answers at the end.

This theme offers yet another reason to learn everything you can about the doubts and fears you are likely to face in offering your persuasion proposition. Good listening will get you to some of that information. But guessing can be helpful as well. Ask yourself, what about my proposal is most likely to raise doubt, fear and uncertainty? What will those doubts be? What is there to fear? What is the cause of the uncertainty? Then organize what you have to say around asking the questions likely to arise, and answering them persuasively.

For example, your proposition is that your company can save money and improve its brand by going green, finding end users for company waste, identifying multiple uses for recycled products, and developing energy alternatives to increase efficiency and cut costs. You would be safe in assuming that there will be many unanswered questions about how all this is supposed to work. Do what you can to anticipate the questions your audience will have in mind. Ask yourself, if I were hearing about this for the first time, what questions would I have? Then ask and answer these questions in your presentation.

One of my favorite ways to facilitate meetings and teach skills with small groups is in a Question and Answer format. I give a little background on what I can do for the group. Then I ask for any questions they may have about how to improve themselves and the way they interact. I write the questions down on a flip chart or white board, and then underline each question before answering it, and cross it off after I'm done answering it. This gives me the pleasure of being more spontaneous in what I do, and creates a more intimate experience for the entire group.

Inoculation

The inoculation theme is a great choice whenever you are certain to face opposition in a group environment. I'm surprised that it isn't used more often in persuasion. It seems essential to me when you know that someone is going to attack you. Instead of playing defense by waiting for accusations and then trying to explain yourself, you can organize what you have to say around framing what your opposition has to say and responding to it.

You can use this to protect yourself in advance of attacks. Tell your intended audience what accusations are likely to be made, or what your opposition is already saying, what objections are likely to be expressed or have already been expressed and are likely to be expressed again, and what your opposition is likely to say or is already saying in response to your proposal. Then tell your intended audience what you want them to hear when they hear the accusations, what you want them to think when the objections are raised, and what you want them to remember when the opposition presents itself. But make sure your inoculation is weaker than the coming attack.

That's right. Be gentle. No need to attack back. Your weak defense of yourself early on can spark your persuadee to a vigorous defense of your proposal later on. In this way you take charge over the language surrounding your proposal, and shape the experience of the people who will inevitably witness the opposition.

Model

A model is a construct that boils complexity down to a simple idea. Models don't have to be true, but they do have to work. Whenever you hear that there are 'four ways to do something, or three possible outcomes, or five kinds of something else, you're hearing a model. Whenever someone shows you a square with four corners, a triangle with three lines, a circle, or a set of five colors, or 9 types, you are looking at a model.

I organize my difficult people presentation on The Art of Communication around the Lens of Understanding model. This model says that there are four good reasons behind bad behavior, and that speaking to those reasons gives you a powerful vector of approach. In my Art of Living program, the Triangles of Health model provides the skeletal framework on which all the material hangs. The hypotenuse of the triangle is an indicator of quality of life. The longer that line, the higher the quality of life. In developing this book, and my live presentation on the subject, I used a model called the 'Countdown.'

Models work, because they create order out of chaos. Models are learnable. And if they work, models are useful.

Components

Think of the component theme as a way of assembling multiple parts into a coherent whole. When you have more than one idea, product or service to introduce to your persuadee, you can use different themes for each component of your proposition. You might use a timeline theme to develop your proposition, and then switch to a model theme to present it. You might begin with a features benefit theme, then go to an Answer the Questions theme, and finish with a model. Or you might start with the Inoculation theme and end with a Story.

The big challenge is creating your transitions from one component to the next. In your preparation for using this theme, identify what seems to you to be the most engaging and interesting order. Then find something in each component that you can use as leverage to introduce the next component. At the end of your presentation, assemble all the components together with a review.

Now it is up to you

The opportunities are limitless for positive persuasion outcomes when you organize what you have to say using themes. And one of the best ways to use themes is to try several on your proposition before settling on the one that you find most persuasive. Try that with your persuasion proposition right now, and then meet me in the next chapter to explore signals of persuasion that are almost irresistible!

15

DELIVERY GUIDES

We continue in our exploration of how to talk in a persuasive way. Here are eight delivery guides to help you take your persuasion proposition to the next level.

The KISS principle

"Be sincere. Be brief. Be seated." Franklin Roosevelt

In the realm of persuasion, do you know what KISS stands for? Not keep it simple stupid! That's insulting! Instead, it stands for KEEP IT SHORT AND SIMPLE! The principle, when it comes to the spoken word, is that you can do more with less.

An example comes to mind. Have you ever received driving directions from someone, and got lost in the directions because of the rich detail they contained? "Go down the road to the first stop light. You'll see a convenience store on the left. Keep going. There will be another stoplight, followed by a stop sign in front of a video store. Keep going." Doesn't that make you want to shout, "Please! I will (keep going) if you don't (keep going)." Far more persuasive, then, to keep it short and simple!

My wife markets an all-in-one liquid nutraceutical product. You may ask, "What's a nutraceutical?" It's a pharmacy grade nutritional product. I'm certain, as is she, that this product would be great for you. But there's a problem with it. It is so comprehensive, offers so many benefits, and she has so many testimonials about those benefits, that she is faced with the temptation to tell you everything whenever she has an opportunity to tell you anything.

The idea with the KISS principle is to find the least number of words to deliver the most information, rather than the reverse.

For example, she could tell you that it is a delicious one-ounce drink, taken twice a day, that provides all the essential nutrition you need. Are you interested? She could tell you that, unlike vitamin pills, this product is almost completely absorbed, right into your cells, without needing to go through your digestive tract. Are you interested?

Do you care about the molecular size and solubility of this product? I doubt it, though if you ask, she can tell you. Do you need to know that it costs less than your daily espresso? Not yet, although you will if you become interested in knowing more. Do you care about the company's history? Why would you? Do you want a list of every system in the body that benefits from this kind of nutrition and why? What would you do with that information? The more you hear, the less you might care.

And that's what happens when most people start talking. They go on and on about how fantastic something is, and with every word, they lose more interest. So here's the point. The simpler the point, the stronger the persuasion.

Now, why should you be interested in her nutraceutical product? No more vitamin pills. Great nutrition. Outstanding results. Any questions?

Two Part Contrast

The human mind employs contrast in order to discern shape, size, color, depth, and design. And two part contrast leverages this mental tendency to make information stand out rather than disappear. Yin/yang. Up/down. Old/Young. Us/Them. Ask not what your country can do for you. To be or not to be. There are two tax systems in this country: One for the informed, one for the uninformed.

One of my favorite movies is Mystery Men. It's about superhero wannabes. It has a great cast, wonderful scripting, and compelling characters. One of the characters uses two-part contrast as a style of speech. His name is The Sphinx, and his superpower is that he is very mysterious. Everything he says employs two-part contrast. He helps the disparate collection of wannabes become a team by counseling them to "Be like the wolf pack, not like the six pack." He helps them grow by advising 'To learn my teachings, I must first teach you to how to learn.' He cautions them 'Hide your strike from your opponent, to better strike his hide.' Hilarious. Effective!

I've used two-part contrast to help patients change self-destructive habits like smoking, or eating to excess. I offer them two compelling ideas of the future. One future is the inevitable result of making no change, with the emphasis on all the negative consequences now and in the years to come. The other is a future freed of the behavior, with all the positive consequences that will ensue. I find that this is far more effective than only talking about the negatives, or only describing the positives. By contrasting the two, you can create a contrasting emphasis that is incredibly persuasive. By presenting the two timelines, I create two synergistic forces for change. I am able to help my patients create some psychological traction with the future that beckons, and some psychological repulsion to the current troubling behavior with a future that frightens. The result is, not surprisingly, momentum for change. That's exactly what I think H. G. Wells was hoping to create for us all when he wrote that 'civilization is a race between education and catastrophe.' Two futures, one choice. Which do you choose?

The Rule of Threes

When it comes to persuasion, there are three ways to get something done: do it yourself, hire someone, or forbid your kids to do it. That is an example of the Rule Of Threes. There is something about groupings of three that just works. Maybe it's because threes help us to remember details. Maybe it's because threes strengthen concepts. And maybe it's because threes organize information into meaningful formulas.

Consider the following threes. Time consists of the (dead) past, the (imagined) future and the present (right now.) Every story, and every persuasive speech, has a beginning, middle and an end. Professional presenters tell you what they're going to tell you, then tell you, then tell you what they told you. Scientific experiments begin with a hypothesis, then an experiment, and finally a result. Sigmund Freud spoke of the id, ego, and superego. The Bible talks of faith, hope, and charity. The Declaration of Independence is built on the values of life, liberty, and the pursuit of happiness, which are protected by a government of the people, by the people, and for the people.

Threes let you set up an expectation, confirm the expectation, and then fulfill it. After all, it only takes two points to make a line. Lines have direction. Direction sets up an expectation. Make your point. Confirm it with another point of the same type. Then drop in the third point of the same type and it becomes memorable. The first point introduces an idea, the second point validates the idea, and the third point proves the idea. The most compelling arguments, the most memorable slogans, and the most profound ideas are delivered using this rule. The Rule of Threes is easy to follow, easy to remember, and easy to act upon.

The Rule of Threes is a favored delivery form for comedians, who use it in a similar, yet different way. The first joke begins a direction, the second joke validates the direction, and the third joke violates it completely! For example: My wife loves my laugh. My daughter loves my smile. My insurance company loves my money. Not that funny? Well, I never know if people are laughing because my material is funny, or because my delivery is funny, or because I make them feel funny. Still not there? Ok. I do know this. There are three kinds of people in the world, those who can count, and those who can't. Moving on.

Rhetorical Questions

So, should you use the rule of threes in your persuasion proposition? The answer is yes. Should you use the rule of threes all the time? No. Should you use the rule of threes to illustrate rhetorical questions? Absolutely. Because when people hear a question and an answer, they find the answer more believable and correct than if it was merely a statement.

However, there is a time and a place for everything, and it isn't all the time and every place. (That was an example of Two Point Contrast!) If you constantly use rhetorical questions, you run the risk of being recognized for the terrible mind reader that you actually are. That leads to frustration and disagreement. And you won't hear most of the disagreement because you're busy talking to yourself using rhetorical questions.

Donald Rumsfeld, as Secretary of Defense under US President George W. Bush, used a litany of rhetorical questions every time he gave a press conference, before, during, and after the campaign to 'liberate' Iraq. If you're asking me did it work, I'd have to say, yes, considering how long he kept his job in spite of his failed management of the war. If you're asking me did it work well, I'd have to say no, because he failed to notice and act on the feedback being offered to him from outside this closed mental system. But if you're asking me 'Should I use rhetorical questions?' my answer is still yes, but only as seasoning, not as the sole substance of your persuasion proposition.

Repeat and Restate

I want to talk with you about repetition. The idea that you can repeat something. Say it a different way. Put into a new frame of reference. Find another way of saying it. Give people a different way of hearing the same thing. Say it over like it's new. Make the same point again and again. Using different words with the same meaning. I'm talking about repetition. Repeating yourself. Restating what you've already said.

In advertising, some say that it takes seven exposures to an idea before it is internalized. In sales, this is called building response potential. That's where you tell someone that you're going to tell them something shortly, but then you don't tell them. Then you tell them you're about to tell them. But you hold off on telling them. If you repeat this pattern three times before telling them what you're going to tell them, you will have more of their interest and attention.

Repetition allows time for your persuadee to have greater comprehension and deeper consideration of your idea. And when you say the same thing in different ways, you create the impression that he is hearing something new, while merely reinforcing the same idea. It's like the motto at Dizzy Dave's Diner. "Our food is tasty, yet delicious!"

There are a few things to keep in mind when using repetition to spice up your Persuasion Proposition. First, remember that a little repetition leads to a lot of persuasion, but too much repetition leads to frustration and aggravation. This fact is familiar to many parents, who can recall a voice in the back seat on a family drive asking over and over again, "Are we there yet? Are we there yet? Are we there yet?

Make Your Point Obvious

I've said it before and I'll say it again. Changing minds is easier than reading them, because most people make terrible mind readers. Tell a story with an unclear point, and they will begin to hallucinate freely. Their hallucinations will prevent you from moving forward, because you are no longer talking with them or to them, but at them instead. Have you ever had the experience of hearing a story and wondering why? Sometimes a story has no point. If you're a great storyteller, sometimes not telling the point can make a story more compelling. But if there is a point you're trying to make, consider making the point first, then illustrating it. Or, simply make the point explicit at the end of your story. Here's an example.

I had a dream. I was flying over a jungle in a small aircraft. The plane landed on a runway hidden in the jungle. I disembarked from the plane, and immediately found a jeep, with keys in the ignition. I looked in the glove box and found a map. I perused the map. It had many details. But it did me no good at all. What's my point in this story? I didn't tell you. But I can tell you by adding the following sentence. I realized that no matter how good the map, if you can't find your location on it, the map is useless.

Or I could add another sentence to the story: All the information in the world serves no purpose unless you know what the point of it is.

Be Directive

Give people a direction. Ask for an outcome. Ask for what you want. The most powerful and persuasive communicators you've ever listened to were the ones who directed your attention, directed your thoughts, and directed your actions. They were directive, instead of waiting for you to be reactive. We discussed this earlier in the book; so let this serve as a reminder. Most people really haven't given much thought to direction, and everyone knows what they don't want. In lieu of a direction, the mind will fixate on what it doesn't want. That's true about you, and true of your persuadee as well. But you get an entirely different outcome when you ask people to define a direction. And you will get another outcome when you require yourself to begin with an end in mind. Then you can tell them where you're going to take them, or tell them what you'd like to have happen, and instead of getting lost in thought, they can simply follow you to find out where they and you are going. The more specific you are about a direction, the more likely it is that things will move in that direction. Direction persuades, particularly when it is the only real alternative to fight or flight.

Use Vivid Language

You've heard it said that a picture is worth a thousand words. But what is a picture worth that is painted with words? It's called an example, and examples, along with the access language of the senses, makes it possible to create and share a vivid experience. Examples add reality to what you say, by providing texture and flavor. I'd like you to think of an example as a sort of brief human-interest piece. It has a main idea or point, which you can state at the beginning of it. Then you illustrate it with a vivid description. Then you restate the point of it. At no point does your persuadee have to wonder why you're telling it to them.

Numbers and statistics have a different impact on your persuadee's thought process. While statistics have some appeal to the logical listener, emotional listeners tend to tune them out or get lost in them.

That doesn't mean you can't have fun with numbers. For example, an engineer, a physicist, and a statistician were moose hunting. After a short walk through the marshes they spotted a HUGE moose 300 yards away. The engineer raised his gun and fired at the moose. A puff of dust showed that the bullet landed 6 yards to the right of the moose. The physicist realized that there was a substantial breeze that the engineer did not account for. So he aimed to the left of the moose and fired. The bullet landed 6 yards to the left of the moose. The statistician jumped up and down and screamed, "We got him! We got him

Or maybe you've heard the story of the man who drowned? He was crossing a stream that had an average depth of six inches.

That's just one of the problems with statistics. They fail to deliver a persuasive message, in part, because of the low opinion most people have of them. It is a fact that facts are stubborn things, while statistics are generally more pliable. Benjamin Disraeli wrote that there are three kinds of lies. "Lies, damned lies, and statistics." This is evidenced by the fact that figures don't lie, but liars figure. You can torture numbers and they will confess to anything. And statistics mean never having to say you are sorry.

More to the point, statistics are far less compelling than examples, because examples are easier to comprehend and understand than statistics. Tell me that carbon emissions have increased by 0.2 percent in 2005, and I may or may not notice that as a meaningful distinction. Tell me that this increase means more asthma and allergies, I may get a little interested. Tell me about a child or senior who has asthma, and describe what it's like not to be able to breathe freely, I may feel moved to reduce my carbon footprint.

That's not to say that you should never use statistics. Statistics can help you move your persuadee in a particular direction. But data without examples virtually guarantees an unpersuasive proposition 99.999% of the time (I made that number up, but you get the point.) If you must use statistics, then illustrate them, because examples are personal, emotionally engaging, and therefore persuasive.

Now that we've put numbers in their place, here are some numbered guidelines for the use of numbers in your persuasion proposition:

Statistics should support your point, not the reverse

If you don't account for the numbers you use, your persuadee will. When designing your persuasion proposition, do not start with statistics and then develop your points from them. Start with your points and then find supporting data.

Sometimes it is better to round off. Sometimes it is not.

Of course, there are times when exact figures are needed. Science demands it. Good engineering requires it. For example, it would be irresponsible for an engineer to say "The bridge needs to be, oh, about...several thousand feet wide. That way it will hold thousands of cars." But you don't always have to be exacting, and that is particularly true when you use a lot of numbers. Rarely will anyone remember 45, 273, 945.653. Better, perhaps, to say "Upwards of 45 and a quarter Billion." And when you can, make that number a percentage (less than half of our products) and then, if appropriate, reduce it further to "four out of every ten of these products."

Translate general numbers into personal numbers.

If my state senator tells me that he is proposing a tax cut or tax increase of $55 million dollars over the next 5 years," it sounds like a lot, and I have no idea how to make sense of it. But if he tells me that this will amount to an additional $15 dollars a year, each year, on my property tax bill, I can understand the actual impact of it. If my wife tells you the price of her product, she has no idea what you'll compare that to. But if she makes the comparison for you, (about the price of your daily espresso), you make the sense that makes it sensible.

Turn numbers into ideas

Make numbers relate to everyday ideas rather than additional abstractions. If you're describing the size of a thing, and you tell me how many yards long it is, I may have to work at it mentally. The result that I come up with could be different from what you intended. Translate that into how many football fields would fit into it, and I'm more likely to understand what you have in mind. Quarts become juice boxes. Pints become beers. And lost pounds become lost inches around the waistline or hips.

Turn numbers into pictures

An animated graph or chart can help your persuadee to understand and retain your numbers. With modern soft-

ware, you can animate a graph or chart so that your persuadee can witness growth, decline, advance, expansion, or
consider your numbers as a tasty pie. If you need to provide
even more detail, do the right thing and write it down, put it
in a handout, and provide it after you are done talking.

Now it's up to you

I'd like you to take 20% of your next 2 hours, and
apply this chapter to your persuasion proposition. Then
close your eyes, and count to ten, before you find me in the
next chapter, where I will woo you and wow you with my
wit and winning ideas!

16

FUNNY PERSUASION

I confess. I find it funny that I'm about to tell you why humor is such a great tool in the art of persuasion. It just seems so obvious. After all, humor speaks in universal truths about human existence, and invites people to laugh at themselves and even laugh with others at themselves.   Or laugh at others in blissful ignorance that the joke is really about themselves.

As I say quite often, "United we stand, but divided, we can't stand each other!" Humor breaks down the barriers that keep us divided and polarized. Humor builds bridges to bring us together. Humor attracts interest, puts people on common footing, and creates an atmosphere of goodwill that is conducive to meaningful communication. Humor discharges resistance, overcomes stubbornness, and creates opportunity for dialog. Humor has such a positive impact on people that more and more businesses (not the dead-serious ones though!) use it to train and retain employees. Educators use humor with their students in order to increase participation and comprehension, and to make the process of learning more enjoyable. Humor is a powerful tool for the change artist. Humor is persuasive.

What's not to like?

But let's be honest. Not all humor is equally funny. In fact, bad humor is also one of the fastest ways to put people in a bad mood, undermine relationships, create hard feelings, offend sensibilities, poison an atmosphere and destroy what could have been a great event, project, team, business, or community.

Some years ago, I attended a dinner sponsored by a professional association to which I belong. The keynote speaker, a member of the professional association, was introduced as a comedian who happened to be 'one of us.' He proceeded to deliver a comedy set that was so shocking, so offensive, and so destructive of the professional atmosphere created by three days of meetings and hallway connections, that people got up and left the room having barely touched the expensive food they left on their plates. He kept going while wave after wave of people left the room. I found it amusing that this speaker failed to notice the result he was getting. I guess you could say he killed his audience, but not in a good way.

Those of us who stayed to watch the spectacle began speculating on how anyone could be so oblivious to what was happening! Maybe, we speculated, he thinks the food was poisoned, and everyone needs to use the restroom at once. Maybe he's nearsighted, and forgot to wear his glasses. Maybe this is his act, to offend as many people as possible, and when he gets home, he'll tell his wife "I killed 'em!' and she'll pat him on the back and say "Great work!" Maybe he had an unstoppable belief in the philosophy that 'If you can't laugh at yourself, laugh at other people!" But none of our explanations came close to accounting for the

fact that he kept on going until the person who had introduced him finally succeeded, after a brief argument, at
pulling him off the stage. That was actually funny to watch,
because he refused to leave several times before she got him
to notice the booing, leaving, and other signs of dismissing
that his bad act had done such a good job of creating. The
lady who introduced him could have used a vaudeville hook,
but all she had were her persuasion skills to get him to stop.
While I don't know what the magic words were that got him
to stop, I could guess: "Quick, CNN is waiting to interview
you in the lobby!" or "That big guy in the front row said
shut up or he'll break your legs." Whatever it was, he did
eventually stop. A few of us were left to notice.

I'd say that it is safe to say that not all funny is funny
to all. And you can't please all the people all the time. Wit,
according to the dictionary, is a combination of perception
and intelligence. So just how do we use our wits to keep our
wits about us? How do we use humor in our communications in order to foster goodwill, camaraderie and common
ground? How do we persuade with humor? There are a few
simple guidelines.

The 55/38/7 holds true

Nonverbal humor makes verbal humor funnier. A
nonverbal lack of humor can make verbal humor as flat as a
pancake, flat as a board, as flat as a tropical ocean on a hot
windless day when the sweat pouring from your skin is hot
enough to make tea but you have no water to drink because
someone convinced you that taking a walk under the cloud
cover that is now gone would be great exercise, and you
shout to the heavens 'THIS IS A VACATION? DEAR
LORD, WHY DO YOU WANT ME TO DIE?????" and
your anguished cry has no echo and falls flat and the silence
makes the heat seem even hotter than had you said nothing at
all. But I digress.

The point I'm trying to make is that verbal humor, without nonverbal humor to support it, can be risky business, like writing that previous sentence. It was really funny when I was saying it, but you couldn't see me. All you have are the words. In fact, one of the un-funniest things you can try to do with words is write about what is funny. It's painful! But the good news is, pain is funny. Keep laughing at me or with me and I'll explain in a moment.

While there are inherently funny words, (NOOCULAR instead of nuclear, for example) you will find more funny in a facial expression, a playful voice tone, and an exaggerated gesture. Yet you can use words to create a funny picture, to imply an accent, or to demonstrate that you have plenty of attitude. Youse got a problem with that? Y'all need me to draw you a pitcher? Let's break it down. I'll use cartoons and TV shows as a way of accessing the pictures in your mind to add life to my hollow words.

There are at least four or five classes of humor, maybe seven or eight. And at first glance, they may not seem to be that funny.

Like pain. Pain is funny.

Comedians understand that pain, whether physical or emotional, is what's so funny about humor. Not all pain. Just the kind you survive. If you're old enough to recall the first few seasons of Saturday Night Live, remember Mr. Bill? (If not, do a web search. It's worth it!) This was painfully funny to watch. People (me) felt guilty about laughing! Mr. Bill was a claymation of a small being, whose limited range of expression included a mouth that went from flat to round, and eyes that went from round to flat. He was tormented by Mr. Hand, who was a hand accompanied by a kind and generous voice. Each time Mr. Hand told Mr. Bill what he had in mind, he made it sound like Mr. Bill would have a lovely time. Only each time, the lovely time was torturously funny. Mr. Bill would scream, in this tiny little voice, 'NO, NO!' but Mr. Hand would never take NO for an answer. You knew that Mr. Bill would somehow survive, so it was funny to watch and listen to the pain of his torment.

Just as it was somehow funny to watch and listen to Elmer Fudd expressing his pain with a speech impediment while trying to catch that wascal wabbit Bugs. No matter how hard he tried, Elmer's every effort backfired on him. The same was true of Wile E. Coyote who, bombs in hand, chased after the elusive Road Runner. But Elmer and Wiley lived on, even after anvils dropped on their heads and their bombs exploded in their pants. And you laughed. Hah!

There's the character played by David Spade in the movie 'Tommy Boy,' Richard Hayden, who turns to walk through a door, and walks into it instead. And Tommy Boy, played by Chris Farley (who was just plain funny to watch no matter what he said or did) says "Holy Schnikes! That's gonna' leave a mark!" Ha! Pain is funny.

Pain is funnier when it is happening to someone else. Not so much when it happens to you. Except, that is, for the people who watch it happening to you. They may be quite amused. They're thinking that it's better you than them. They are laughing at your expense. Nice of you to give them such a treat. Which gives us a new twist on an old adage. "If you can't laugh at your own pain, laugh at someone else's."

Unpleasant surprises can be funny

Unpleasant surprises can be very funny if you have fun with them. Johnny Carson built his career on the unpleasant surprise. His jokes, for example. The unpleasant surprise was that this late night entertainer with a highly paid writing staff could tell a joke that wasn't funny. But the audience loved when Johnny's jokes didn't work. Johnny laughed laugh at himself, and the audience laughed at him too!

This taught some of us that you could be funnier if you make a mistake, a great relief to professional presenters who do screw up on occasion. If I flub a word in front of an audience, I make fun of myself and my audience laughs. Why? Because they don't expect a highly paid professional speaker to have trouble talking. I laugh at myself, and they laugh with me, and we share the joy of my embarrassment.

If you've ever told a joke to a group (and I have), and the joke bombed (and it has,) you know what I mean by an 'unpleasant surprise.' It's that moment when you expect to hear laughter, and instead there is just the sound of your own heartbeat, thumpthump, thumpthump, and maybe a few people talking to each other trying to explain the joke. But if you then make a joke out of your botched joke ("Trust me, you'll thank me tomorrow!" or "Don't make me come out there," suddenly it seems that your joke is funny after all!

What's funny about unpleasant surprises? Technically, you could say it is incongruence with expectations. Although saying it that way isn't funny. Well, actually it is funny when you say it out loud! Incongruence with expectations is funny! HA! All that means is that if you expect me to step up, and instead I fall down, you may try not to laugh out loud, but it will probably strike you as funny. Not as hard as it will strike me, but funny nonetheless. Indeed, this is the essence of the punch line. (Punch, get it?)

James Thurber defined humor as "emotional chaos remembered in tranquility." In other words, something that wasn't funny at the time is, in retrospect, hilarious. Because it is so incongruous with expectations. HA!

A play on words can be funny.

There are all kinds of ways to play with words, including accents, puns, malapropisms, mispronunciations, or calling something by the wrong name. Like calling your wife the name of a former girlfriend in a romantic moment. Wow, that's funny. You would have laughed had you been there. I kid.

Phrases can be funny. Deciduous to my species is a funny phrase. Turning a phrase or an idea inside out is funny. Dijon vu - the same mustard as before. A hangover is the wrath of grapes. Does the name Pavlov ring a bell? My friend has a photographic memory, but it was never developed. Caution: Those who get too big for their britches will be exposed in the end. Marathon runners with bad footwear suffer the agony of defeat. Acupuncture is a jab well done. Do you get the point?

Ridicule can be funny

Making fun of serious things can be funny, just as being serious about funny things can be funny. Though in this age of the politically correct, you should be very careful about who and what you make fun of. Ridiculing yourself is always a good bet. There was a time when laughing at 'the other' was funny, whether it was a racial difference or a gender difference.

Actually, gender differences are still funny. This is universal, so everybody gets it. Like that time I was working with a couple in my counseling practice. And the husband says to me, "She's crazy, doc!" I replied, "Funny, she says the same thing about you!" And he says, without a trace of irony, "Well that just proves how crazy she is!"

Timing makes funny

Humor, like beauty, is in the eye of the beholder. And timing is everything. For example, if someone you are walking with trips on a stair, you could say, "Have a nice trip?" and maybe they'll chuckle. Or hit you. Or both. Wait an hour, and the response is likely to be "Huh?" On the other hand, something that isn't funny in the moment may be much funnier in retrospect. Most of our painful memories are like this. Those moments about which we say "Someday I'll look back and laugh." To which I can't help but reply, "Why wait?"

Bad delivery can be funny.

Perhaps the funniest thing of all is when someone butchers a joke. "A string walked into a bar. Or wait, it was a restaurant. No it was a bar. Whatever. The waiter, or maybe it was the bartender, tells the string to leave. No wait. The bartender, yeah, that's who it was, says to the string, "Hey string. You have to leave." No, wait. He said, "No strings allowed." No wait, he points at the sign that says, "No strings allowed." Yeah. Then he says, "You have to leave." And the string is confused." And so are you. That's funny! Not the joke, but the terrible delivery.

Irony can be funny.

Irony is the very soul of humor, though ironically, irony is not always funny. It's ironic, for example, that in a country like the USA where food is plentiful and sex is permissible, the culture appears to be starved for both. That's just sad. But irony is also what you call it when you say one thing but mean something else. You can do this by overstating (hyperbole,) "That was the most fun I've had at a meeting," following a boring meeting. Or, "What a brilliant

145

idea" about the dumbest thing you've ever heard. And you can also use irony by understating (hypobole?). Let's say your friend wins an award. And you comment, "Is that the best you can do?" Or you can be ironic through the use of sarcasm. Peggy Sue 's husband says something predictable, and she feigns excitement. ""I just can never guess what you're going to say next!" Or she says, matter of factly, "Fascinating," when her husband says boring. Peggy Sue may not know that she is being ironic. But a casual observer who finds the husband to be a dim wit would likely recognize the irony. Often, the key to irony is found in a tone that betrays the meaning of the word.

What isn't funny?

If it is tasteless, spare us. Unless you know us and know that our taste runs all the way to tasteless. And really, the only way to know what is and isn't funny is to know as much as you can about who you are talking to and find out what you can about what they find funny.

In-jokes are usually only funny to the people in on the joke, the people who shared the experience with you. They tend to leave everyone else drawing a blank. But sometimes, you tell an in-joke, the people who are in start laughing, and the people who aren't in on the joke start laughing too! All the while, they are wondering, and maybe even saying, "What's so funny?" because they want to know why they are laughing. They're having an unexpected surprise!

And what about sarcasm? Ah, sarcasm. The lowest form of humor and the highest form of wit, or so, some say, said Oscar Wilde, though, of course, there's no proof of it. For the sake of comparison, I daresay that flatulence is the lowest form of wit, and it sure cracked me up as a kid! But consider the etymology of the word sarcasm, from the Greek sarkasmos, meaning 'to tear the flesh; to bite the lips in rage.' Hmmm. That doesn't sound very funny! In fact, sarcasm is often the result of hidden or suppressed anger. And indeed, the cutting edge of this kind of comedy has the potential to cause pain. So the question remains. Is sarcasm funny?

It sure can be. As in, "Ah, I see you've set aside some time today to humiliate yourself in public!" As in, "I like you. You remind me of when I was young and stupid." As in "I'll try being nicer if you try being smarter." As in, "Well, you probably said it without thinking, the way you do most things." As in, "I've had an incredible evening. But not tonight."

Sarcasm has been used to great effect in making fun where there might have been none. During Adlai Stevenson's 1956 presidential campaign, a woman called out, "Senator, you have the vote of every thinking person!" To which he replied, "That's not enough, madam, we need a majority! " It's funny, because it is about everyone, but no one in particular. Well, at least it's not about you. Don't get me started on the joys of watching the fake news shows like The Colbert Report, and The Daily Show, where the clever use of sarcasm provides audiences with enough laughter to make the intolerable news of the day at least a bit more tolerable.

Sarcasm aims at a target. And it is not always funny, unless it is used the way I use it. I use sarcasm when talking about other people who first use it on me. Then, as part of the same stories, I use it on them, and now they deserve it. My audience seems to agree. HAH! But I never use it directly on anyone. Except my former best friend, who tells me that hurtful sarcasm means, "I care about you" in his hometown. I'm not sure if that's true. If it is, he must care about me a lot. But then, if he had an honest opinion, it would probably wind up be in solitary confinement. My biggest regret is that, when we were friends, I could never quite lower my I.Q. enough to have a meaningful dialog with him. He's inscrutable, like a Vulcan, only without the ears, or the depth. But I hear that a mind reader offered to read his mind for half price! I kid. He's a great friend. And say that with only a trace of irony in my voice.

By the way, I used to think that the single best response to sarcasm was "I know you are, but what am I?" I've since learned a funnier response. Take the sarcastic remark at face value, as if it is meant to be exactly what it says. Someone tells you "Do you tie your own shoes?" You reply, "Yes, as a matter of fact, I do." Keep that up and after awhile, they'll take their sarcasm and go away. "Don't let the door hit you on the way out!" you can yell helpfully after them!

Let's review:

> **Pain can be funny.**
> **Unexpected surprises can be funny.**
> **A play on words can be funny.**
> **Ridicule can be funny.**
> **Timing can be funny.**
> **A bad delivery can be funny.**
> **Irony can be funny.**

Ok, so that's how humor works. But how does humor work when you seek to persuade? The persuasion guides will help you. Kiss. Contrast. Threes. Rhetorical questions. Make the point. But here's the point. If you follow a few simple rules, you may surprise yourself with how funny you are. Better yet, your audience may share in your surprise!

Funny Rule #1: Find your own funny

First, you have to find humor in your own funny. If you don't, your persuadee won't. But if it makes you laugh, or brings a smile to your face, then your persuadee can, at the least, enjoy your enjoyment of whatever it was you thought was so darn funny. My wife derives this kind of joy from my sense of humor fairly regularly. She constantly tells me, when I'm laughing at my jokes and silliness and she isn't, that, "I'm happy that you're so easily entertained. "

Sometimes, the best funny is unintentional. Notice it, appreciate it, and do it some other time on purpose! My best material was the stuff that happened accidentally. From then on, it happens accidentally on purpose!

I went to a surprise party for a friend the other night. He just turned 70, and he's a bit of a mentor to me. And I was asked to stand and say something. I said "One thing I appreciate about Hal. Whenever I feel like I'm getting old, I go and spend some time with him." The audience laughed. Then I figured out what they thought I meant. I could have explained that I was impressed with his youthfulness, but hey, I went with the joke instead.

Funny Rule #2: Point to a point

Second: Stay on message. Unless you're just building some rapport before presenting your persuasion proposition, persuasive humor isn't just funny for funny's sake. You don't want people scratching their heads trying to figure out what you intend, so tie your funny to your proposition.

That's not really hard to do. Ever hear of junkologic? It's an advertising principle discovered in the 1940s and 1950s. Someone figured out that you can take two unrelated ideas, and act like they're related, and people will find a way to relate the ideas as if they were! How else do you explain ads that show smokers sitting next to their bikes on mountaintops in pristine wilderness areas? Even if your funny and your point aren't actually related, they become related the moment you say they are.

Funny Rule #3: Short works better than long

Go on too long and people may hop in their thought-mobile and mentally drive away. You don't want your persuadee losing patience with you. Better that you think of funny as punctuation rather than paragraphs. Quick one-liners and the occasional play on word are usually funnier persuaders than long stories that have no point.

Funny Rule #4: Timing

It's all about timing. And to develop your sense of comedic timing, you've got to put your funny to the test. If you can, try it out on a few people, notice their reaction, work on your timing. In fact, almost everything funny about funny is dependant on timing. Appropriate timing means you don't make fun out of people that are struggling emotionally. There's a time and a place for it. Although you might be surprised to find that most people appreciate a good laugh, even when life's got them down.

Good timing means waiting long enough for people to get the joke. Remember to slow down a little when you get to your punch line. How much should you slow down? Slow enough to say these words to yourself. "Wait for it. Wait for it." And remember to punch up the punch line with enough emphasis that people get that it's a joke. Get it?

I went to a political fundraiser. Our state representative was being introduced by a former local politician and now local radio personality. Our state rep is well liked, and was a key speaker at the fundraiser. Here's how Jeff started his introduction. "When I first began organizing this event, I talked to so and so in the state capital. I had to listen to her go on and on about how great our representative is, and all that gets done, and what a great speaker he is, and more, for about 45 minutes." He said this slowly, and he rolled his eyes, and made a face as if having to hear about an effective legislator was painful for him. In fact, the reverse is true. Everybody laughed out loud at the irony. The timing couldn't have been better.

Funny Rule #4: Never telegraph your punches

Punch lines, that is. I learned this lesson from Captain America. If somebody knows what's coming, they won't find it nearly as compelling as when you take them by surprise. And in the art of persuasion, you don't want to be a comedian. Comedians have the hardest job in the world. People know the comedian is supposed to be funny, so they have the attitude of " Go ahead. Make me laugh." That's a lot tougher than getting people to laugh when they're not expecting to! In my line of work, my audiences come in with a "Make me learn" attitude instead. And instead of making them learn, I make them laugh, and then sneak the lesson in while they're laughing. The point: Never say that you're going to say something funny. That way, if it turns out that it's not that funny, nobody will be the wiser. Unless you make the joke that nobody was the wiser. And if it is funny, people will have that pleasant surprise that makes funny work so well.

Now it's all on you

Ok, kiddo, go have some fun with funny, and while you're at it, make your persuasion proposition funny too! If it was already funny, make it funnier. If it's not funny, be ironic. Then walk, don't run, to meet me in the next chapter to discover the persuasion signals that make your proposition almost irresistible.

17

SEVEN SIGNALS INTRODUCTION

Why are some people more persuasive than others, even when their facts and evidence are flawed or don't hold up to scrutiny? Wouldn't it be great if everyone were logical, reasonable, and thoughtful?

Well, we're not! According to Ellen Langer, a professor in the Psychology Department at Harvard University, people are cognitive misers. We're stingy when it comes to thinking. In fact, we conserve our energy by avoiding thinking whenever and wherever possible. Why? We have at least a few very good reasons.

First of all, critical thinking, or thinking things through, is not encouraged in most cultures and countries in the world today. Political and religious authorities essentially advise people to 'do what we tell you to do, and don't question us, because we know what we're doing.' And in spite of all the evidence to the contrary, people are mostly willing to take this advice!

Second, there is some speculation that our brains lack the capacity to keep up with modern life. According to the people engaged in this speculation, outside of hunting and gathering, we are under-qualified for deep thought. There is plenty of evidence to support this. We even have a name for it, The Peter Principle, that goes roughly like this: In hierarchical systems, people tend to rise to the level of their incompetence. Although, ironically, I can't help notice that this could mean that the people doing the speculation about our brains may be under-qualified to draw conclusions!

Third, according to some research, thinking hard creates the same brainwave patterns as actual physical pain. (My brain hurts just thinking about that!)

Perhaps the best explanation is that thinking is energy expensive. That's right, thinking actually burns 3 times as many calories as not thinking. Specifically, 1/10 of a calorie per minute is burned when your brain is in a resting state, and that jumps up to a dramatic 1.5 calories per minute when you do a crossword puzzle or contemplate the meaning of life. Of course, that's far less than the 4 calories a minute you burn when walking. But we live in a sedentary society, so it's not all that meaningful of a comparison. Thinking this through, if you can walk and think at the same time, you can burn more calories. But if you're not walking or thinking, which is apparently the case for many people, you'll probably conserve a lot of energy, and therefore gain a lot of weight!

So the next time you hear a politician telling you that their work is hard work, it is possible that they are only referring to the great effort involved in thinking. I find it interesting that the people who make the most money in our society burn the most calories, either physically (athletes) or mentally (professionals like doctors, lawyers and investment advisors!) Athletes also get paid to make us feel like heroes and winners when we cheer for them *and* they win.

No matter the reason, the evidence is clear. People conserve thought energy whenever possible. We look for shortcuts to save on having to think. We listen for cues to save on having to think. We avoid thinking unless it's absolutely necessary to do it. When a decision has to be made, we say, "What do you think?"

Here's an example. A stray cat adopted us awhile back. He showed up in our carport, and won our hearts by rolling over and over when we looked at him, reached for him, or otherwise engaged with him. We named him Rollie, a name that didn't require a lot of thought. Initially, my wife set up a cardboard box with a blanket in it, on a table in the carport, so he would have a place to sleep at night. This lasted a week, at which point she decided that he ought to just live in my office. I was happy to share my office with Rollie the cat, but I didn't want my office to smell like a cat. My office needed work anyway, so I decided to remodel it and give Rollie his own entrance and some private space in the closet. We hired a contractor, Mike. He tore out the doorframe, and gave us the assignment of visiting the local lumberyard to select the new door that would go next to the panel containing Rollie's entrance.

So we're standing in the gaping hole where my door used to be, and Mike says, "Rick' did you have a chance to look at the door catalog at the lumber yard?" I replied, "Yes, I did, but frankly, there were a lot of doors in that catalog, and they all looked more alike than different to me." Mike asked me if I had picked one. I had to tell him, "Mike, I couldn't do it." He says, "It's your office, you need to pick a door." So I turned to my wife, and I said, "Honey, what kind of door do you think I should have?" And she said, "It's your office, you decide." I replied, "I know it's my office, but I couldn't pick one. Mike, what door do you recommend?" Mike said, "It's your office, you have to decide." So I looked at Mike and at my wife, and I said, "Look you guys, I know it's my office, but I need help here. Mike, if it was your office, what kind of door would you pick?" And Mike laughed, and said, "I would have to ask my wife."

Do you understand what was happening? None of us wanted to think anymore about the door than was necessary! And that's what I mean when I say that people conserve thought energy.

When we don't want to think, how do we decide things? Emotionally! We make decisions based on the fact that someone we respect is the one who gives us information. Or we like someone. Or something 'seems' better. Or we feel like we owe somebody something. Or we started down this road, might as well go all the way. Or everyone else is doing it, so we figure it must be right. Stock market and housing bubbles anyone? And how else do you explain why people keep buying computers that run buggy, virus and hacker prone operating systems that are poorly designed, when there are better alternatives available?

I want you to think about this, right now. Even if every one of your brain cells keeps crying out TOO MUCH DATA! Maybe there is, and maybe that's what you need if you're going to be a master persuader. So relax, and consider this key idea. There are two ways that people can listen to you when you speak, LOGICALLY and EMOTIONALLY. When a person listens logically, they are interested in facts, details, and other high quality information that they can use to evaluate what you are saying.

When people are busy, overwhelmed or tired, (which is most people most the time,) they pay attention for cues and signals that tell them what to think without having to think about it. That means that more often than not, your persuadee is listening emotionally. Am I saying that most people are thoughtless most the time? Nope. In fact, most people are thinking about something most the time. Sex. Food. Sleep. Self-esteem. Status. Survival. But unless a person has grown up with a lot of support for critical thinking, you can expect to be talking to someone who is listening emotionally a good deal of the time. It just isn't enough to have the facts on your side. You've got to be able to speak to people who are barely thinking!

For our purposes, there are seven of signals that such people are looking and listening for, and it is possible that they work because our nervous system is designed to respond to them. Indeed, according to Robert Cialdini these seven signals have tremendous social value for us, and we may be genetically programmed to heed their siren call.

Here's the thing. I'm going to tease apart that which is often found together. In other words, it is a rare situation to find only one of these signals in play. More often, two, three or more or working together, even though little is being said. But by teasing them apart, I hope to make them obvious and unmistakable to you. These signals are triggered multiple times a day, and you respond to them. In the next seven chapters, you'll learn how to trigger them in others, and how to protect yourself when they are triggered in you. Why is it important to protect yourself? Because your mind has a bad habit of going on automatic when you most need it to stay on manual!

When people are overwhelmed, don't have time, don't have enough facts, these shortcuts are engaged. There's nothing wrong with that. Each cue has positive social value. But not always in the way it is applied. Ultimately, how you use these signals depends on your own integrity and ethics. My conscience is clear.

I want to give this information to you. I can't wait to give this information to you. A nice person like you should have this information. So onward, dear friend, to the first signal, Affinity.

18

THE SIGNAL OF AFFINITY

Here's the windup, and here's the pitch.

Hi. I'm Rick. Mind if I call you (fill in your name here)? I'm a husband, father and businessperson. I've worked with a lot of people just like you for quite a while now. And I know a little something about how it is for you in dealing with the world around you.

I know that sometimes, when you offer your ideas, it seems like no one is really paying attention. I know that sometimes, you try to make something better, but people seem determined to make things worse. I know that when you see a problem, you wish people would put more into solving it than complaining about it. I know that you want to help. But the fact of the matter is you need help. I get it! That's why I created The Art of Change Skills For Life™.

You like people who are like you.

We are more likely to be persuaded by people who we recognize as similar to ourselves than by people who lead with their differences. Come on, admit it. When you meet someone for the first time, don't you size them up to determine if you can relate to them, connect with them, maybe even trust them? If they share your background, or have work in common with you, or you have mutual friends, or agree about anything that you value, that raises the affinity quotient.

Some people possess a great deal of affinity with others. They resonate familiarity and approachability. Maybe you call it charm, or charisma. Maybe it's just energy and enthusiasm with a smile. But there's something in their smile, something in their manner, and something in their concern that tells you that you're dealing with someone who is somehow like you, or at least the way you'd like to be.

You like attractive people.

The ugly secret is out. In our society, it is generally true that we admire handsome and pretty in others. Attractive is more desirable than strange and ugly. Ironically, over the last several years, at last a few people have begun at last to notice their own strangeness and ugliness, and embraced it. As a result, strange and ugly has developed into an attractive subculture for people who feel strange and ugly.

People on juries like attractive people more, and believe them more, than unattractive people. In action movies and comic books, heroes are handsome and bad guys are hideous. If you usually dress down, but occasionally dress up, people will notice it and comment on it, right? "Well, you fix up nicely," they say, and give you a warmer greeting than usual.

You like people who like you.

Some people have a lucky charm, acquired early in life, when they learned that you get more from people by building them up than from tearing them down. So charming people give lots of praise and compliments instead of criticism and condemnation. And the result is that people tend to give them more appreciation, more opportunity, and even more of a break when things go wrong. My mom always said, "You get more flies with honey than with vinegar." Why you would want the flies, well, that she never mentioned. But she also taught me that there's always something you can appreciate about almost anyone. You can appreciate them coming, or you can appreciate them going. You can always find a reason to give an honest compliment or authentic appreciation, even if it's nothing more than "Thanks for being so honest about how you feel."

You like people who treat you with respect.

When you treat people with respect, you create more affinity. You know how it is. You tend to prefer people who seek to understand, who are willing to hear an opposing view, and who consider you as important as they consider themselves. This is also true institutionally. When businesses treat customers with respect (for their time, their ideas, their interests), they become preferred providers. When customers prefer a business, the business prospers. When businesses treat employees with respect, they become desirable work environments. Respect engages the affinity factor, and affinity is a powerful persuasion cue.

You like what people you like, like.

Well-liked people trade on their likeability. They become spokespersons and do product pitches, so that their likeability rubs off on the product or idea and creates affinity for it. Celebrity endorsements are a perfect example of this. Whether it's the hair coloring, "Because I'm worth it," or the soap ad with the attractive stranger who says "Aren't you glad you use (product name)? Don't you wish everybody did?" are designed to elicit from the audience the response of "They're like me!" or "I want to be like them!" When a movie or TV star goes public with a political position, they are hoping to loan your liking of them to the cause they believe in, so that you will like their cause. Word of mouth advertising works on the affinity signal as well. If someone you like tells you about something, you may be more inclined to like it too!

How to send the affinity signal:

It's easy! Point out common ground. Treat people with respect. Show an interest in their interests. Get other people who like you to give testimonials about you, and create positive associations between your proposal and your persuadee's favorite projects, people and ideas.

How to protect yourself from affinity signals:

When someone tries to take advantage of your affinity with him or her, here's how to protect yourself from possible bad intent. It's easy! Just think for yourself! Notice what is being asked of you, and separate it in your mind from the person asking it.

Did you like that? Was it better than you expected? Had enough or want more? Because it just keeps getting better. Meet me in the next chapter to learn about the signal of Comparison!

19

THE SIGNAL OF COMPARISON

Here's the windup, and here's the pitch:

What if there was a simple way to get everybody on the same page about just getting along with each other? What if it was possible to get the people in your life to be more proactive and less reactive? What if there was a way to decrease conflict and increase creativity instead? You would want to know about that, right? Well, that's why I created The Art of Change Skills For Life™!

That's the signal of Comparison

Comparison: To consider one thing in the light of another. Compared to worst, bad isn't so bad. Compared to great, good isn't good enough. Compared to bad, good is pretty good. And compared to good, Great is freakin' awesome! And that is how comparison increases the value of your persuasive proposition.

Your nervous system is designed to make comparisons. When you're cold, you jump into a hot tub. Then you're hot. When you get out, the air seems warm, or even cold! (Here's how to stay warm when getting out of a hot tub on a cold day...put an ice cube in your mouth while you're still in the hot water. That will distract you from the air temperature as you get out of the bath!)

Compared to what?

The sign on that plasma TV says 'Regular Retail, $4399. Today, only $3179. You'd be crazy to pass up a deal like that. You say, "Holy cow, I'm saving money!" as you spend it. Why? Because now it seems so reasonable, in comparison!

My wife is constantly saving us money by spending it. I don't know why I can't find any of that money she saved! But she just loves to get a good deal. Really, who doesn't? After all, it's built into us! And how does she know it's a good deal? How do you know it's a good deal? By comparison.

Why did you buy your house? Compared to all the others you looked at, maybe it was a palace! Although compared to a palace, maybe it is a fairly modest house. But then, who looks at palaces when shopping for a home? Maybe you looked at more modest homes than the one you bought. Whose idea was that? The realtor! Maybe your house was the last one she showed you, and the best of the bunch.

Professional speakers like myself know that it can make a difference who you follow up to the podium. Put someone up there who bores the audience to tears, and the next speaker, with even a little savvy, will come off great. Put someone up there with energy, enthusiasm and a stellar delivery, and the one who follows could pale in comparison.

In both cases, it could be the same speaker who follows! I've been asked which I'd rather follow, a great speaker or a lousy one, and my answer is always "I'd rather follow a great one!" Why? It's all about my motivation. I like a challenge!

Start with a benchmark

All you need is a benchmark to stabilize the judgment of the person you want to persuade. Years ago, a friend and I made a series of ads for our local public television channel based on the comparison of a pledge drive or no pledge drive. The gist of it was "Send us your money and we won't do a pledge drive!" Funny thing about it was that our series of ads was a pledge drive! But we made it fun, made it funny, made it interesting, promised that if it worked, there would be no disrupting of your favorite shows. And, unlike a regular pledge drive, we got it over with fast. "You can pay us now, or you can pay us later." And it worked!

Comparison can be good for you, or bad for you, depending on the benchmark you use as a reference point. Want something to look good? Compare it to something that looks bad. Want something to seem smart, compare it to something dumb. Want something to seem affordable, or even cheap? Compare it to something expensive.

The FLINCH is a nonverbal comparison

Comparison is the foundation of buy low, sell high. When selling, start high. Then when you come down, it is easier for your buyer to say yes. When buying, start low, so your slightly improved offer seems like a better deal. In negotiation, this principle is behind a tactic called 'the flinch!' If you offer me something and I immediately accept it, after you've had some time to think about it, you'll be thinking you could have gotten more for less.

I taught the flinch to my daughter, when she got her first big writing job. It was a great job, and it came with a full boat of benefits. She wanted the job, no question. They wanted her, no question. The only question was money. I told her that no matter how much they offered her, to look disappointed and say she was hoping for more. That little flinch was worth several thousand dollars a year. What could it be worth to you?

Consider the order of comparison

There is an ideal order for comparisons, and the best way to know the best order is to know what you want to leave in the mind of your persuadee. If it is fear, end with fear. If it is desire, end with desire. If the answer is a positive direction, end with that. Mark Twain put it this way. If you've got to eat two frogs, eat the big one first. If you want to get a yes response, make a bigger request first. Then, if it gets a NO, make a smaller request, and you may find it gets a YES because it seems so much more reasonable or doable. Can you donate three hours every Sunday for the next six months? Nope. Can you give us an hour this Sunday? OK. Researchers on persuasion have found that when a big request that gets a NO, following it with a small request is likely to get a YES. One study showed that in fund raising, such a sequence of personal requests for donations increased the amount raised.

Implied Comparison

Comparison can be implied. When you read, or hear, or someone tells you that something is New & Improved, what's implied? That the previous version is now old, oh, and by the way, compared to this model, the old one didn't work so well. When someone says a thing is better, or faster, or more enjoyable, what is the implication? The implication is that there was something worse, slower, and less enjoyable. Want to start a new trend? Highlight the failures of the people or groups at the head of the old one. This implies that your new direction seems better in comparison. Want to stop a new trend? Highlight the failures of people or groups that have refused to keep up with the crowd. This implies that the old way of doing things is better in comparison. Nothing more needs to be said.

Invite a comparison

Making a comparison is not the only way for a comparison to be made. Considering that people conserve thought energy, sometimes a comparison is too hard to follow, offers too many details to adequately consider, or requires too many assumptions on the part of your persuadee. In such a case, instead of making the comparison, invite the comparison. An invitation includes a request. "If you put these two payment plans side by side, you will recognize that my plan offers more flexibility and payment options than my competitor. "If you compare these two products, you will notice that my product offers many benefits that the other product cannot."

The beauty of this approach is that, more often than not, people will be more inclined to take your word than to make the comparison themselves. If you compare making a comparison to inviting a comparison, I'm certain that you will see that inviting a comparison is the quickest and easiest way by far to send the comparison signal.

Size Matters

But be warned. Too much of a comparison, like too little knowledge, can be a dangerous thing. Big comparisons can polarize people into their positions. Compare great to awful and it isn't believable. Compare awful to fantastic and you're likely to hear 'it can't be that bad.' And if what you are offering is too far out of the range of a reasonable comparison, you're likely to hear "I'd rather stick with the devil I know than go with the devil I don't." The way to prevent that from happening, the way to stay in the acceptance zone, is to be incremental rather than dramatic. Small changes don't seem as significant, and thus get a smaller reaction of good or bad, instead of terrible or amazing. That's how the Fed raises interest rates. That's how your insurance company raises your premiums.

How to send the Comparison Signal:

It's easy! Start with a benchmark. Then compare something to it! The order is based on what you want to leave in a person's mind. You can ask for a lot and then ask for a little. You can imply a comparison, nonverbally with a flinch, or by highlighting the failures or successes of people leading a change or championing the status quo, or by using comparative words like more, better, faster, new and improved. But remember that if your comparison is too big, the impact will be reduced. Incremental comparisons take you farther.

How to better protect yourself:

When someone tries to take advantage of you by making comparisons, here's how to protect yourself from possible bad intent. It's easy! Separate the items being compared one from the other and consider each on it's own.

That applies to real estate (what do I think of this house, not in comparison to others, but on its own merit,) business opportunities (what do I think of this opportunity, not in comparison to others, but on its own merit) or ideas and proposals (what do I think of this idea, not in relation to others, but on its own merit).

I did my part, will you do yours?

Now if you liked this chapter, I think you'll love the next one! But the only way to find out is to turn the page just like everybody else. Next up, CONFORMITY!

20

THE SIGNAL OF CONFORMITY

Here's the windup, and here's the pitch!

If you are frustrated with the pace and direction of change, you are not alone. If you are tired of dealing with pompous fools who don't have a clue, you're not alone. If you wish you had a better work environment and a more fulfilling life, you are not alone.

And if you choose, you can join with hundreds of thousands of people all over the world, people just like you who have decided to quit waiting for change and to take their destiny back into their own hands, Hundreds of thousands of people dealing with problems just like yours, who have decided to do something about their situation instead of wishing things were different or hoping their problems will just go away. You are not alone, and you don't have to go it alone. That's why I created The Art of Change Skills For Life™!

Pull together what other forces try to pull apart

The desire to conform to a larger group is a deep-seated impulse that explains much of the human condition. In fact, the tides of history are awash in conformity. Communities, cultures, and collections of people moving collaboratively towards common goals, common clothes, and against common foes. This desire is built right into us, part of our basic design. This same desire is the instinct that serves schools of fish in turbulent water, flocks of birds flying in formation, and packs of animals surviving in the wild! Think it through and you'll see that it's true. We want to be part of movements and forces greater than ourselves, and for good reason. Our ability to survive as a society depends on our ability to work together, to be together, and to move together towards the greater good. If we always acted like a herd of cats, everyone going in their own direction, society would be hard pressed to solve any of its problems. We invent social institutions to keep us pulling together even when forces work to pull us apart.

You tend to do what others are doing

The urge to merge presents itself when survival is at stake, but also when it is not. When I was a kid, blue jeans were all the rage. If you were a nonconformist, you wore them (just like all the other kids!) to show you were different. Their popularity continued to grow, and today people in every generation all over the world wear jeans and love them. Maybe because in their mind they conform to some idea about identity (rugged individualist, cowboy, working stiff, casual personality) that each person comes to on their own (or through relentless advertising!) It happened with espresso, Walkmans, and iPods. From Beatle haircuts to racing cars, from sports shoes and golf clubs to clothing and fashion, conforming to trends is, and always was, all the rage. Top hats. Mustaches. Bicycles, then cars. Washers and dryers. Speakeasies. Nightclubs. Smoking and drinking. Not smoking. Drinking health drinks.

One day, my wife and I were walking through the big park in our small Oregon town. As we moved past the playground area onto the walking paths that meander along the stream and into the forest, we noticed a handful of people standing and looking up. We couldn't help ourselves. We had to stop and look up too! "What are we looking for?" we asked, as we stood and stared in what appeared to be the right direction. "There's an owl in that tree," said one of them excitedly. "Where?" We really wanted to know. "Up there," she gestured. We looked and looked, and finally, after ten minutes, we thought we saw it, blending in to the tree, and watching us watching it ever so wisely. Then we looked around, and saw that the crowd looking up had grown some. Five had become fifty, and most of them, I'm guessing, had no idea what everyone was looking at!

We attended a seminar in Chicago a few years back. The room was packed with eager participants, each dreaming of making a fortune buying and selling houses, land and buildings. The seminar leader exhorted us to go for it, because there was opportunity all around! And without a trace of irony, he then told us about the 'Moo, Bah' syndrome, the propensity of people to act like herds of cattle and sheep. I noticed as I looked around the room that I wasn't the only person looking around the room and wondering if others had detected the seeming contradiction.

In 1992, Michael Hammer, father of the reengineering movement that swept through the business community, wrote an article in the Harvard Business Review in which he said, "It's time to stop paving the cow paths, obliterate them and start over. " Do you know what a cow path is? Out here in the west, cattle are allowed to graze in our state and national forest lands. As a result, if you like to go camping,

170

you will come across cow paths from time to time. My advice is, if you follow a cow path, walk carefully. I did.

Having read Hammer's article, I once decided to follow a cow path and see where it led. It didn't go anywhere in particular, but instead it meandered all over the place. And I found myself wondering why the cattle kept changing direction. After all, there was no apparent reason when the path shifted, no insurmountable obstacle, no barrier requiring it of them. And then I realized, the cows were simply following the leader, and the leader had no direction! The changes in direction were the result of a few cows wandering in the same general direction, and the other cows basically deciding, 'Oh, ok.'

In light of this experience, I gave some thought to Michael Hammer's statement, and realized a meaning for it. You see, the difference between cows and people isn't the meandering, the following of leaders who don't know they're in front. We have such things in common with cows. The difference is, when we change direction, we institutionalize the change in direction and conform to it. We pave it over with certainty that it must be right, because nobody is saying anything other than 'Oh, ok.' That's the power of conformity. That's why we don't always produce the best decision. We conform to the first decision when it seems everyone else is going along with it!

Change is conformity on a bell curve

Fortunately, change also happens because of conformity. That's what happened in the USA with a woman's right to vote, and then with civil rights, and then with the banning of cigarette smoking in public places, and espresso booths at gas stations. Now it's happening in healthcare, education and governance. The change brought on by conformity happens on a bell curve. It starts with early adopters, those people on the leading edge of a trend, the crazy ones as Apple put it in the Think Different ad campaign that signaled the beginning of their turnaround. These leaders are simply following their own inner guidance, doing what they think is right. They are seen as dreamers and fools by the vast majority of people, who are still following the preceding trend. But in time, a few more brave souls follow the early adopters, who are then followed by larger and larger groups that come to the realization that, hey, maybe those dreamers are on to something. They are watched in turn by the larger group, the vast majority, who publicly think those dreamers are nuts, but privately think 'hey, maybe they're on to something.' Eventually, they join the trend, which is now unstoppable. Before you know it, you've got everybody on board except a small group of luddites and stragglers, dummies and dinosaurs if you will, who never got it, don't get it, and will never accept the change.

But the dummies and dinosaurs also seek groups with which to conform. When I began writing this book, there was a meeting of holocaust deniers in Iran. And like dinosaurs, these conforming creeps may never get it, but they will eventually die off. Dinosaurs demonstrate a great reason not to wait around for everyone to get on board when you're working to change something for the better. Don't let the dummies and dinosaurs doom your change efforts. Sometimes, you have to get something started, and hope the wisdom of it is enough to draw the attention of early adopters. The rest follows naturally.

Popular is persuasive

Conformity isn't just about conforming to the crowd. Sometimes, it's about popularity. I do not hesitate to use what works when promoting my various enterprises, and neither should you. When I'm giving a speech, the person introduces me as a bestselling author. Why? Because it's in the introduction I provide, and it is there for the purpose of getting the audience, who has yet to hear me and may know

172

little about me, to think 'Wow, he must be great, otherwise why would all those people have bought his book?'

Why do we have polls? To tell us who is winning so we can back the winner. People figure the winner must be doing something right or he'd be a loser like the other guy. Even if the reverse is true, that the loser is a winner and the winner is a loser, it's what the crowd thinks that determines reality. It must be funny, everyone's laughing. It must be a moving sermon, everyone's putting money in the hat. It must be a credible diet, everyone's following it. It must be an attractive fashion, because everyone's impressed. He must know what he's talking about, everyone is deferring to his judgment!

Problem is, the person at the front may not know anything you don't, or may not know something you do! What if they are mistaken? So following the crowd can, like your mother told you, get you into a world of trouble. People may wind up following the leader, like lemmings, going over a cliff. That's the situation with Conventional Wisdom. It purports to reflect the majority view. But more often than not, it is an out of date view, and out of touch with what's really going on.

How to send the conformity signal:

It's easy! Help people see, hear and think about your idea as part of a growing trend, a popular movement, or at the least, something that others have done successfully. Find your allies, build a small group to get the ball rolling. Identify and cultivate early adopters. The more you bring on board at the outset, the more will join in as you move forward. No one wants to stick their neck out, and gamble on losing it. But they'll eagerly follow the crowd to find out what's going on or be part of the success that they expect as a result of their conformity.

How to protect yourself from just going along:

In order to conform to what I've said in each of the previous chapters on persuasion signals, I must say it again. Think for yourself. Is it right for you? Snap out of the moo-bah. Look up. Look around. Then use your own best judgment. You may wind up going another way, and find yourself at the head of the crowd!

Everyone's doing it. Now you do it.

How can you add conformity to your persuasion proposition? When you've got it figured out, turn the page. I'll be waiting for you in the next chapter! And I'm saving you a place, so you can learn about the signal of RECIPROCITY.

21

THE SIGNAL OF RECIPROCITY

Here's the windup, and here's the pitch:

I could have kept this to myself, but I've found the skills and strategies that anyone can use to change just about any situation or relationship for the better. And I want you to have them. All I'm asking of you is to do yourself a favor, and take advantage of my work. And then there's one thing you can do for me. I want to share this with as many people as possible. So if it's not too much trouble, would you please tell people about The Art of Change Skills For Life™? Would you do that for me? Thanks!

Do for others and they'll do for you

Reciprocity is all about a little give and take. When someone gives you something, some part of you knows that you should give something back. Give a little, get a little.

Quid quo pro. I rub your back, you rub mine. I favor doing you a favor, if you'll do one for me in return.

But what does it mean to do someone a favor? A favor implies that you are acting against your own interest in favor of theirs. It implies that you're making a sacrifice of some kind. As a favor to you, I'll watch your back. As a favor to you, I'm giving you a great deal. As a favor to you, I won't tell anybody. As a favor to you, I'll let you go first. As a favor to you, I'll treat you with respect even when you fail to treat me with respect. And when you look out for other people's interests ahead of your own, they have a reciprocal tendency to look out for your interests in return. Imagine that. Look out for others, and they will look out for you.

Give a little, get a little

Sometimes, people really do want to help each other out. Sometimes, strangers do care, and the willingness to sacrifice is innocent and authentic. And sometimes, these patterns get played out in the big leagues by heavy hitters, and nobody sees it coming until the game is over and the losing team retires to the dugout.

Have you ever had this happen? A car salesman takes your case to his boss to "see what I can do for you." The clothing store clerk helpfully steers you towards a rack of incredible suits, in limited supply, that happen to be on sale. Pretty decent of total strangers, wouldn't you say? It is entirely possible that these helpful strangers are setting you up for a string of recommendations that will cost you far more than the pretty penny they saved you when they made you their mark! The car salesman comes back and tells you of his valiant effort on your behalf, then earnestly encourages you to purchase the undercoat, an overcoat, and a maintenance plan to protect your valuable purchase from the elements. The clothing store clerk thinks it's a shame to get such a nice suit without the right (and expensive) accessories. "You wouldn't want all that beauty to be wasted."

I will if you will

Horse-trading is another way of describing reciprocity. In negotiation, it's the trading of concessions that leads to the negotiated outcome. And as any good negotiator will tell you, there has to be some trading with every concession, or the negotiations will grind to a halt. But the rule of concession making must be obeyed, or you'll lose more than you gain. Never make more than one concession at a time. Wait for the first one to be reciprocated before offering the next one. Conditional trades lead to conditional trades, and that's how you arrive at the mutually satisfactory result.

You can put this signal on your side in the presentation of your persuasion proposition. Be ready to go first, give first, offer first, and share first if you can do it as a favor or concession. Do this with no (obvious) strings attached, and you just may find that your persuadee wants to discharge the obligation as quickly as possible by giving something back. Will you take yes for an answer?

Free for you, free for all

One of the fastest ways to create this effect is offer something for nothing. The word free triggers can trigger the desire for reciprocity. The free dime attached to the survey that comes in the mail. The free address labels that come with the request for money. The free calendars, the free vacation rental at the time share, the free sample of the product are all intended to create some obligation in those who accept the gift. That's the funny thing about free. It often isn't. The one making the offer knows the desire to accept a free gift is incredibly powerful. Powerful enough to obligate you into doing something in return.

No doubt you've met a few successful sales people who were unbelievably unlikable. How do they stay in business? How do they succeed? By creating a string of obligations. Fact is, an inconsiderate jerk can steal a client away from someone who is friendly and attentive, if the jerk can find a way to obligate the client first.

Nobody needs a guilt trip

Of course, it is possible to use reciprocity badly. When you have strings attached to a 'favor,' your obligation creation may send people on an unpleasant guilt trip, creating resentment and the desire for distance instead. But done sparingly, and without attachment, a little sacrifice at the outset can lead to a splendid time for all (what with all the giving and receiving going on!)

How to send the signal of reciprocity:

It's easy! Let me do you a favor and repeat what I've been saying all along. Give a little, get a little. You rub their shoulders, they rub yours. You offer something free; they want to balance the account. You make a sacrifice or offer a favor; they want to balance the account. Quid pro quo.

How to protect yourself from a scratched back:

It's easy. When an offer is extended to you, think! Make sure you open your eyes at the same time that you open your hand to receive, so that you're not disadvantaged by your eagerness.

Don't get me wrong. I'm not saying that you shouldn't accept gifts. Gifts are great to give, and great to receive. But there are times when it is good to question whether what you are receiving is an honest offer or if you are being treated as an advantage waiting to be taken. Does that mean that you can't trust the intentions of others when they offer to do positive things for you? What a shame it would be to miss out on the benefits of legitimate favors. Here is a useful approach to handling a free gift, a favor or a sacrifice. If someone really wants to give you something, let him. Since giving and receiving go hand in hand, and sometimes the greatest gift we can give is receiving another's gift, you can consider yourself even, just like that! No debt, no obligation, they wanted you to have it, and you did them the favor of letting them give it to you.

If guilt is your problem, let me do you a favor and tell you about my e-Book on 'Dealing With Relatives.' It contains a number of powerful strategies for staying off the guilt trips. And if you order today, I'll include my powerful article, absolutely free, on Dealing With Adolescents! (Really, I will! Because I want you to have it!) New Rule, kid. When it's trick or treat, treats can be accepted. Tricks don't have to be.

Say, could you do me a favor and turn the page? There's something important I have to tell you in the next chapter! You don't want to miss it. You can't afford to miss it. You better not miss it. It's called Authority. So get moving!

22

THE SIGNAL OF AUTHORITY

Here's the windup, and here's the pitch:

I only talk about what I know, and people who have worked with me will tell you that I know what I'm talking about. So believe this. Studies show that individuals who develop their behavioral persuasion skills, enhance their creativity, live purposefully and learn to work well with others are more likely to lead more fulfilling lives, be better parents and spouses, win more awards and recognition, effect more change and make more money than people who don't. And that's why I developed The Art of Change Skills For Life™!

Obedience to authority

Obedience to authority is one of the basic lessons in almost every culture in the world. Lessons in obedience, and the consequences of defiance, appear in holy writings and scriptures dating back to the dawn of civilization. We are culturally conditioned to be obedient, we are taught that honor and duty go together, and we find reinforcement throughout our upbringing, in the form of rewards for obedience and punishment for defiance.

This conditioning works! The Milgram experiments of the 1960s demonstrated that people will do what they are told to do, even if they think it is wrong, as long as the person telling them to do it is considered to be in a position of authority. More recently, the Abu Graib prison scandal revealed the same forces at work.

Having someone in authority serves in a few important ways. It tells us who to follow in a crisis, or when facing uncertainty. Authority also gives people cover for their actions, which may explain the occasional eagerness of others to do what they are told. Because when something is wrong or goes wrong, those who've made someone else the authority can claim they were only 'following orders.' When someone puts you in charge, it may be because they don't want to get stuck holding the ball.

Authority is an important persuasion signal. You would be well advised to pay attention to it, learn about it, and use it. But how do you project an air of authority? And how much of the signal do you send before it creates a backlash?

First impressions count, and only rarely do you get a second chance to create one. I've read and believed that you have between two seconds and two minutes before that first impression is complete. Not a lot of time, and so much depends on it. A first impression tends to be based on appearance, credentials, perceived experience, and the people with whom you associate, along with the authentic authority you convey in the way you talk and behave.

The appearance of authority

People do judge a book by its cover, and they judge you based on your appearance! Numerous studies have been done on the influence and persuasive power of appearance. Uniforms convey social authority. They tell us who to follow, who to listen to, who to obey. They create a sense of power and authority in those wearing them, too. When an athletic team takes the field, the entire community can vest its pride in their uniform. But if you don't have or wear a uniform, a nice suit can make a difference! Studies conducted on the influence of appearance consistently demonstrate that appearance counts. One study involved a man approaching strangers on the street and asking to borrow money. Some times he was dressed in a suit, other times casual clothing. He was loaned more money while wearing the suit. Why? People who gave the stranger money had more confidence that it would be returned. When he was wearing casual clothes, he was just another guy asking for money.

Another study compared the influence of a well-dressed person crossing a street against the light vs. a casually dressed person doing the same thing. Researchers counted how many pedestrians followed the example of each. No surprise, the suit carried more leadership ability when it came to breaking the law.

Students give higher ratings to professors based on appearance. Daniel Hamermesh, a professor and doctor of economics at the University of Texas, says that appearance can make a 12% difference in earning potential. Professional presenters learn to dress a little nicer than their audience. Why? If you dress for success, you appear successful. Dress down from your audience, they are likely to feel superior to you, and give less credence to what you have to say.

Is this always true? No. Some people feel more comfortable around comfortably dressed people. But in general, people respond to appearance and grant some authority to those who pay attention to it.

The color of your clothing can convey some degree of authority, or so say numerous image consultants. According to them, dark implies authority and power. Navy blues and olives, the same colors as uniforms, may give you at least the veneer of power. Black, the darkest color of all, is so powerful that it often appears stark, cold and unfriendly, and people who wear black may want to emphasize their affinity signals to create some balance for the purpose of persuasion.

Of course, it is possible to influence what people think of you in spite of appearances. There is a story dating back to the 1860s regarding President Abraham Lincoln. He was attending a party, and as people recognized him, they began to comment to each other on his appearance. Someone said, loud enough for him to hear, that "He is a very common-looking man." Lincoln's reply: "The Lord prefers common-looking people. That is the reason he makes so many of them."

Experience conveys authority

If you have experience, speak from it, because experience counts. A strong brand name for your company means authority travels with you when you represent that company. If you or the group or idea you represent have any standing at all, then by all means, stand on it. People who have been in the same business for many years know that experience counts. Business people tend to prefer doing business with tried and true performers rather than eager new upstarts who have no track record to back their ambitions and claims. Experience brings with it wisdom. Wisdom carries authority. Is this always true? No.

Some people have years of experience from which they never learn. Some people have no wisdom, just lots of evidence for the limitations they carry through life. And some people prefer the excitement of youth, the greater willingness to take risks, and the capacity for creative thought and action one finds in the person who dares to be naïve over the tried and true. But a track record of positive experience is more likely to convey authority than the lack of one.

Associations convey authority

However, even when you lack experience, if the people who support you have it, their experience can grant you some degree of authority. In the 1980s, when I was in my first year as a full time speaker and trainer, I was one of only 15 presenters at the world's then-hottest training company to be chosen by the Tom Peters group to present Tom's revolutionary 'In Search of Excellence' material to the business community. Even though I was a newbie in the corporate training world, I carried Tom's authority with pride wherever I went. His authority gave me authority. It opened doors, and lots of them.

Tom used to say that the person with the biggest Rolodex wins. At the time, it sounded interesting, but I didn't fully understand the implications. Now that I'm older (much older,) I realize the power of our associations and the experience and authority those associations contain. More often than not, it is not what you know, but who you know that counts. People who know the right people can have a strong front, because they know someone is watching their back. And with experience comes connection, and through our connections we gain access to possibilities that otherwise might never come to us. As we act on those possibilities, our network grows. And the size and quality of our network, the cumulative authority and experience it contains, may determine our future.

Authority by degrees

In our society, it is understood that people who have invested their time, money and energy in pursuit of higher learning have demonstrated a certain level of commitment. We honor degrees and titles, because we value education, and such achievement conveys authority. Does everyone feel this way about education? No. Some people feel more comfortable with people who have the common touch, and they perceive the use of titles as arrogance and superiority. But in general, people respond to titles and degrees, and grant authority to those who possess them.

I earned my title of doctor (N.D.) from a four year naturopathic medical school, following three years of pre-medical education, and I use it whenever I first make contact with a business, whether as a customer or as a service provider. In the initial moment of contact, it does make a difference. For example, when I book a hotel room, I'm certain to say 'Dr. Kirschner.' Yet sometimes, you need to draw on the authority of others.

One night, I arrived late at a hotel, and the desk clerk informed me that they were out of rooms. "But I have a confirmation number," I exclaimed. "Yes, but we have no more rooms," came the reply. Undaunted, I drew on higher authority to gain some staying power, as in 'staying in the hotel that night!' I said, "If the President of the United States needed a room here, right now, would you have one for him?" "Yes," he said tentatively. "Well, he's not coming. I'll take his room!" He laughed, and gave me a room.

Beware of fakes and phonies

The authority of a title has become so desirable in business and society that degrees are losing their connection to the experience they are supposed to represent. In the last two decades, diploma mills have sprung up like spring flow-ers across the land, using 4 color glossy magazine ads to market coveted titles in exchange for little work and much money. For example, in unlicensed states, fake ND degrees are sold to people wanting to play doctor for a few thousand dollars. Anyone can play! Spammers, likewise, send mil-lions of invitations to unsuspecting and ignorant people looking for a shortcut to the authority they themselves rec-ognize as inherent in an earned title. But why do people fall for these valueless degrees, and send their hard earned money to con artists and societal bottom feeders? Maybe they aren't thinking clearly. More likely, they desire author-ity but lack the character to legitimately pursue it.

Pardon my rant, but this is one of my pet peeves. This kind of deception is bad business for society, as it dam-ages public confidence and undermines education. In those states where diploma mills are tolerated and fake degrees go without challenge, legislators have the authority and respon-sibility to protect their constituents. I hope one day they will. Until then, one can only hope that the posers with phony de-grees drop out to avoid scrutiny, or are found out and their façade crumbles.

Ironically, you don't need a degree to have authority. Not if you have authentic authority.

Authentic authority

It is a common misunderstanding that the true mantle of authority is granted by an outside agency, by degree or pedigree. While you may judge a book by its cover, you may eventually read the book. And either there's something to it, or there's not. There are many titled people whose foolishness, arrogance and ignorance earn and get them nothing but derision from peers and strangers, and whose lack of real authority guarantees that their pronouncements and proclamations carry all the gravitas of a helium filled balloon.

The authentic signal of authority gets sent in subtle and not-so-subtle ways, and begins on the inside, and then manifests on the outside of who you are. Clearly, if you don't respect your own authority, you will be hard pressed to impress others with it. The way you present yourself to the world speaks volumes about the regard in which you hold yourself and your views. So the question you need to answer is, who grants you your authority? And the answer, ultimately, is that you determine the value and worth of your own experience and ideas. After all, how can I respect you if you won't?

Confidence conveys authority

Confidence comes from preparation, and confidence conveys authority. Speaking with authority is necessary if you intend to lead another person or a group to a decision, idea or action. The way you walk and talk tells the world whether or not you respect your own authority. It comes across in the way you enter a room, and when you leave it, when you sit at a table and when you stand in a door, the strength or weakness of your voice, the degree of congruence in your expression. Because I spend a good deal of my time in front of groups, I've learned to speak clearly, to enunciate, and to project my voice to the back of the room. The side effect of this is that the way I talk to groups has carried over into my personal life. My wife says that whenever I talk, I just sound like I know what I'm talking about. She enjoys the irony.

There are other ways of boosting your credibility and having more authority behind your persuasion proposition. I refer here to evidence and testimony.

Rules of evidence

Evidence, if it is favorable to your cause, grants you authority. If it is unfavorable, it undermines your authority. For the logical thinker, strong evidence is the most powerful persuasion signal of all. But when people are thinking emotionally, it's not the quality of evidence that counts most, but the quantity of evidence that conveys authority. The more evidence you offer, the more authority you convey, because a lot of evidence is more persuasive than a little.

Think back to some of the big televised trials of the last century or this one. Remember all the expert testimony, the mounds of evidence? Both sides try to drown the jury with detail, in order to convey the impression of having truth on their side. And at the end of the trial, it isn't a matter of common sense, or fact, or logic. An impression is formed about the quantity of evidence and testimony, and a judgment is made. In this way, the guilty walk and the not guilty are imprisoned.

Pick a side

They say there are two sides to every persuasion proposition. What you would speak for, someone may be inclined to speak against. But research demonstrates that if you have a strong proposition and your persuadee is already inclined to support it, you will be more persuasive by only providing the evidence that supports your proposition. You design this one sided presentation in order to gather and reinforce support, by providing credible facts, credible people who support those facts, and credible reasons to support your proposition.

However, if the case against your persuasion proposition has possible support, and your persuadee is not leaning one way or the other, you will find more persuasive power in presenting both sides of your case, the evidence for and the evidence against. Using the power of inoculation, you can present the evidence against and then refute it, undermine it, and frame it as you like. You can counter the evidence with other facts, undermine the credibility of opposition, and frame your opposition using the strategies discussed in the Opposition chapter. Then present the evidence in favor and support it with authority.

Studies show

Whenever you say 'studies show,' only rarely does someone ask you to show your studies. I still encourage you to only cite studies that are real, because the power of trust overrides all others in the art of persuasion. But whether the studies you cite are real or not, well designed or not, relevant or not, the fact that you offer them as evidence conveys authority to a person looking and listening for the signals of persuasion.

Testimonial evidence

Testimony is a kind of evidence. In fact, there are at least two kinds of testimonial evidence. There is expert testimony, where someone in the know or someone who should know says that something is so. And then there is the testimony of anyone other than you.

Expert testimony conveys authority when you don't have a lot of facts on your side. Someone who is recognized as an authority or expert on the issue or subject to which your proposition pertains can serve as a substitute for having any factual evidence to back you. A recognized expert, speaking on behalf of your idea or proposal, loans you her authority. And, just like with other forms of evidence, whenever there's a difference of opinion, the person with the most recognized experts on their side is likely to be more persuasive to those who have yet to take a side.

Often, you don't need an expert. You just need someone, anyone, to speak on your behalf. This is the Authority of Other, and it requires anyone other than you. Advertisers know this. They hire people you don't know, and have them say things they know nothing about, in order to convince you to think you know enough to buy their products and services.

These days, you see testimonials from people who are missing a first name or a last name being used to promote ideas, products and services. B. Miller says "This was the best one I've ever experienced!" Kathy H. says, "Don't wait another moment! If you want to succeed, you'll find the answers here!" The key is that they look and sound like they have authority, because someone is referencing them! This is particularly effective when the person being persuaded doesn't really know anything about the subject either.

When a stranger in a store overhears customers talking with unsolicited enthusiasm about a particular product, that testimonial evidence may be enough to close a sale. I'm a bit of a geek when it comes to certain kinds of technology. On more than one occasion, I've found myself in a computer store in a town not far from here, listening to a salesperson talking a customer into a cheaper and more trouble computer than what he came in for. I know why the sales clerk does this. His store stands to make more money on customer misery and repairs if they sell the buggy stuff! But I can't help myself. I speak up, I forcefully contradict the salesperson, and offer my opinion. I must be persuasive, because the customer always takes my recommendation over the sales clerk and buys the better computer. To date, I've sold over $65,000 worth of computers. Didn't make a penny on any of them. I did it because it was the right thing to do. Numerous experts would agree with my recommendation.

Here's a useful bit of parenting advice: You can use this with your kids! If they are of an age where they won't listen to your opinion, share with them the opinions of others that make your point for you. My mom was still doing this with me when I was 50 years old. She would read things in magazines, highlight the lessons she wanted me to learn, and send me the articles! My dad had a favorite relative tell me some things about politics and policies when I was a teen-ager.

Some years ago, we were driving up the interstate to visit my in-laws for the holidays, and I had the misfortune to slip on ice in a rest area along the highway. I had a dental emergency. Frantically, I called and asked for a referral to a dentist who might see me right away. For a confessed dental coward, the thought of letting a dentist I didn't know work in my mouth was truly terrifying. When I arrived at his office, he still needed a few minutes to get set up for my visit. I was sitting in his waiting room shaking in my boots, when I noticed a photo album sitting on the table beneath a lamp. Nervously, I picked it up to thumb through it. But it had no pictures, only thank you cards and letters of appreciation, all carefully preserved. The more I read, the calmer I became. By the time the dentist was ready for me, I was completely confident that I was in good hands. Though I didn't know the people who wrote those messages of gratitude, I surely was as grateful to them as if I did.

How to send the authority signal:

It's easy! Dress for success. Emphasize your experience and staying power. Invoke the names of people who will back you. Have others speak on your behalf. You can be prepared, and speak with confidence, stand with confidence, walk with confidence. All of these things serve to create an impression of authority. And once created, it goes where you go.

However a warning is in order here. Some people have trouble with authority. Perhaps you are one of them! If so, you know that if all a person has to persuade with is authority, they should be prepared for resistance. People don't like to be talked down to, they don't care for arrogance and they resist any idea that they didn't think of first. Balance the authority signal with other persuasion signals in order to create true persuasive power.

How to question authority:

When someone tries to sway you with the voice and appearance of authority, here's how to protect yourself from possible bad intent. It's easy! Just think for yourself. When presented with an expert, ask yourself the question, "Is this person really an expert?" Then, ask yourself, "What does this person stand to gain if I'm persuaded? How will this person benefit if I'm persuaded? Once you've answered these questions, you can evaluate what you are being shown or told on it's own merit, rather than simply being swayed by the signal of authority.

You must now apply this material.

You have authority. Where is it? What is it? How can you make it known when presenting your persuasion proposition? You must not go forward or turn the page until you've taken the time to apply what you've just read.

Then, and only then, you will find me waiting, as I have throughout this book, patiently, consistently. Because you can count on me. I have Consistency, and you can read all about it in the next chapter.

23

THE SIGNAL OF CONSISTENCY

Here's the windup and here's the pitch:

The moment you picked up this book, you made an important decision. The fact that you are reading this book tells me that you recognize the value of this material. And as you apply what you read, you make the wise choice take advantage of the research done by others and myself for your benefit. Stick with it, see it through, and I will satisfy any curiosity you might have about what insider's know about the art of persuasion. That's why I created The Art of Change Skills For Life™!

Consistency fulfills expectations

We have every reason to expect at least some consistency in the behavior of others. What kind of world would this be if people constantly changed their minds, changed their values, changed the rules? When I give you my word, it sets a level of expectation. If I keep it consistently, you come to know that you can count on me. After a time and at some point, I don't have to say a word for you to know I'm good for my word. When I tell you I'm going to do something, and then I do it, and then I tell you I did it, and I do that consistently, you come to know that if I say it, I will do it. And, as I said earlier in this book, such trust has tremendous persuasive power.

In a conflicted world and a life filled with disappointments, people want an experience consistent with their expectations. This is the driving force behind some of the best businesses in the world, behind some of the most effective leaders in the world, and behind some of the most powerful persuasion that you've ever witnessed.

Inconsistency leads to dissonance

In the same way that consistency leads to fulfillment of expectations, inconsistency leads to cognitive dissonance. Indeed, we find inconsistency to be disturbing. If the value of a product you purchase is inconsistent with the price you pay, cognitive dissonance leads to a loss of trust. If a salesperson promises the sun, the moon, the stars and the sky, and a transaction takes place, and then the customer calls in to talk to customer service only to find out that "Um, we don't actually do the sun, the moon, the stars and the sky," the cognitive dissonance is great enough to put an end to that relationship forever. And if somebody pitches a persuasion proposition, and then representations made in that presentation turn out to be false, that person will lose all credibility and find it hard, if not impossible, to regain it

Ralph Waldo Emerson was correct when he said that 'a foolish consistency is the hobgoblin of little minds.' It is not always sensible to be consistent, a case John Kerry tried but failed to make in the 2004 presidential election. "I voted for it before I voted it against it, and I'll tell you why."

Problem is, that's the wrong thing to say. A smarter choice would have been, "My votes were consistent with my principles." Consistency is far more persuasive than inconsistency. We associate consistency with personal and intellectual strength, whether true or not. In politics, incumbents almost always get reelected, and not just because of gerrymandering and vote rigging. Voters don't want to admit to a mistake!

Many if not most people would rather stick by bad decisions than have to admit to bad judgment! Inconsistency creates cognitive dissonance. And dissonance drives people to distraction. Most people hate dissonance with such intensity that they try to avoid noticing it whenever possible. Maybe you ignore dissonance and hope it goes away. Or maybe you deny it, and 'stay the course.' Maybe you defend, explain, justify and otherwise make excuses for it, in the hopes that it will seem consistent if you consistently explain it away. Because of your deep dislike for dissonance, you can overlook glaring examples of inconsistency for incredibly long periods of time.

People are not often persuaded by dissonance. They are persuaded when they find that a change is necessary to restore consistency with more deeply held values and beliefs. They are persuaded when the change they are asked to make is more consistent than staying with the same unreliable and inconsistent thing. Yet dissonance has value. It draws our attention and interest to new possibilities. It can force us to solve a problem in order to restore consistency. That's why intentionally introducing dissonance is such a great creativity tool. You can seek out the exception to the rule in order to force a new perspective.

When people are inconsistent, we may quickly conclude that they are undeserving of our interest and support. But given enough time, inconsistent may become consistent. If someone remains consistently inconsistent, perhaps because of a consistent commitment, we may re-evaluate at some point. We may come to the conclusion, that what they are saying or doing is worthy of our interest and support. Think of Apple Computer's 'Think Different' campaign! Apple committed to a campaign that at first blush seemed to champion inconsistency with the status quo. When it first hit the market, their market share seemed to stagnate. Then, slowly but surely, the tides changed. Today, Apple is an acknowledged leader in design, from virus proof computers to plug and play peripherals. This consistent delivery is what allowed them to successfully challenge the 'foolish consistency' of the near monopoly that dominated the market place.

From yes to yes to yes

Confucius said that a journey of a thousand miles beings with a single step. And herein lives the beginning of the key idea for using the consistency signal in the art of persuasion. Life is complex. Issues are complex. Decisions are complex. Consistency makes everything simpler. Once you've made a decision, made a commitment, or made up your mind, consistency means you don't have to think about it anymore. No more weighing the pros and cons, sifting through facts. Simply stay consistent, and you have a convenient and relatively effortless way to deal with complexity. And to get to that point of resolving an issue or making a decision, you have to go from point to point, from yes to yes.

If you can persuade a person to say yes to your first request, they are increasingly likely to say yes to your next request. If you can get an appointment with a decision maker, that decision maker is more likely to hear what you have to say. If he hears what you have to say (and it speaks to his MAP), he is more likely to consider the merits of it. If he considers the merits of it, he is more likely to take action on it. This is called building a YES set. Yes. Yes. Yes. Yes. New idea? YES.

That's the value of getting a person to make a public commitment to something that you can then use to support your persuasion proposition. "You spoke of the importance of a clean establishment in our last conversation. Do you still believe in the importance of this?" Yes. "Then don't you agree that we should do everything in our power to accomplish it?" Yes. "And wouldn't a failure to keep the baseboards clean undermine the overall cleanliness of this establishment?" Yes. "Then can I count on you to task someone with this, so that these baseboards get cleaned?" Yes. "Who will you assign and when will it be done?"

How to send the consistency signal

It's easy! Tie everything you say back to your main ideas, so that your main ideas are woven as a consistent thread through what you say. Treat people in a consistent and persuasive manner, so they come to expect such behavior from you. Be consistent in what you value, be true to your word, and keep your promises and agreements. Let yourself be known by what you stand for, what you represent, what you hope for. If you say you'll meet someone at 2:00pm, be there on time no matter what. Tell people what you're going to do and then do it. Tell them you're going to be listening for a while before talking, and then listen for a while before talking. Tell people what you're going to tell them, then tell them, and then tell them what you told them.

How to stop getting in deeper than you should:

When someone tries to persuade you with consistency, here's how to protect yourself from possible bad intent. It's easy! Remember, the idea is to get a commitment from you, and rely on you to avoid dissonance as long as possible by staying true to your original commitment. So consider carefully what is asked of you. And if you find yourself backed into a corner, or the great deal you thought you were getting becomes very different somewhere along the way, reserve for yourself the power to be consistent to your self interest rather than the deal.

For example: You go to buy a car. There is a low price on the sticker. You jump at the great deal, and then, for some reason, the price keeps getting ratcheted up (It's called up selling, where more and more gets added on to what you've already agreed to do.) You go along with it for a while, even though you can feel the dissonance. Why? To be consistent! The sales person reminds you of previous statements or agreements or actions already taken. But you have the right and ability to think! Ask yourself, if you had known where this was going before you first said yes, would you have made the same choices? If the answer is no, then notice it!

Now it's up to you

As I've asked you in previous chapters, I ask you here to please continue to apply this material to your persuasion proposition. Sure, it's extra work, but the reward for your consistency will be more compelling persuasion propositions than ever! And as soon as you've done this, I'll meet you in the next chapter. But you better hurry. I'm running out of time to write, and pages to write on. And I want to make sure you learn about the signal of Scarcity!

24

THE SIGNAL OF SCARCITY

Here's the windup, and here's the pitch:

I have to talk fast. I want to do something special for you because you made it this far. This is an exclusive offer, and it's for a limited time only. But you'll have to contact me to find out what it is. So don't take too long. It's only for the first 20 people. So what are you waiting for? This moment and this opportunity may never come again.

One last thing. What I am about to tell you is not true for all of us all of the time. But it is true for some of us some of the time. If you intend to use the art of persuasion to change your world, you must act as if this is true most of the time. I'll keep it brief.

People value what is scarce

From the law of supply and demand to the exclusive membership offer, scarcity increases value. It's hard to get what's valuable, and what's valuable is hard to get. When everybody wants something, it's likely to be in short supply. If something is in short supply, everybody must want it. Right?

It's the holidays. There's a popular item. Word on the street is that there aren't enough to go around. Prices skyrocket. You get one. Your friends think you are the luckiest person in the world.

The world's best band is reuniting for a reunion tour. Demand for tickets is huge. An entire industry develops around sold out performances, as scalpers buy large batches of tickets to lessen supply. It becomes the must-attend even of the year. A friend has two tickets he can sell to you. But they're going to cost you plenty!

Less available usually means more valuable

It's not just scarcity of things that increases demand. Scarce intangibles are also more valuable and hard to get. Like time, information and appreciation.

Limited time is valuable

When you don't have much time, your time is more valuable to you, and more valuable to others. The more available you are to people, the less they may value your time.

Privileged information is valuable

The most valuable information is off the record, or incredibly private, or very personal. It makes itself scarce. It hides at secret meetings behind closed doors, and avoids open forums that anyone can attend. It hides in the privileged conversation that takes place between a doctor and a patient, an attorney and a client, a parent and a child. It escapes through a private revelation. And its value diminishes as soon as it is revealed.

Appreciate what is valuable while you can

Appreciation given too easily is little reward. Appreciation given sparely has more value. Easy rewards may entice, but the best rewards are the hardest to get. And don't it always seem to go that you don't know what you've got 'til it's gone. Appreciate what you've got while you still have time. Life is short. Anything can happen. Take nothing for granted.

Privilege and exclusivity create scarcity

Unless you're Groucho Marx, who famously disclaimed interest in being part of any club that would have him as a member, most people love the idea of privilege, whether it's privileged information, privileged admission, or a privileged opportunity. There's something special about being special. It happens so rarely. It has great value.

You can increase demand for something by emphasizing exclusivity, or the sense of competition for it.

Off limits creates scarcity

Like kids who know there's a Christmas present hid high up in the closet, people hate to wait and refuse to be denied. Think about it. How do you respond when someone tells you that you can't have something? "You can't have it," is often followed with "Then I must have it!" The more obstacles, the more irresistible. We seem to be wired this way. Just ask your kids. Toys. TV. Movies. Friends. Food. Dates. You say no? They say yes, which rhymes with 's' as in 'sneaky!'

You: You can't see that him/her anymore! Response: But we're in love!
You: You're grounded. Response: Climb out the window.
You: No peeking. Response: Oops.

Forbidden may seem more valuable than it is.

That's why censorship tends to be self-defeating. Freedom of speech keeps bad information and ideas from becoming valuable by putting them out in the open. You censor an artist or entertainer and the value of their work and views goes up, up up! Consider the case of the Dixie Chicks.

10 days before the invasion of Iraq, lead singer Natalie Maines disparaged the American president George W. Bush during a concert in England. The press picked it up, and the comment made it its way across the USA. All across the land of the free and home of the brave, the Chicks were banned from country radio. But the censorship attempt backfired, as records sold like hotcakes. A movie about their experience, 'Shut Up and Sing,' packed the house, and is doing well on DVD. The reaction to the reaction seemed to be, "There must be something in what they are saying that you don't want me to hear. I've got to listen." The ban literally became the band's brand.

Scarcity has a language of its own

The language of scarcity is urgency and importance, privilege and prestige, prohibition and forbidden fruit. "Ends this Friday!" "Five Days Only!" "The next 23 people." "Last chance!" "Don't miss out!" "Scandalous!" "Private Now Public" "First time ever!" "$1000 pizza, complete with caviar!" "Available exclusively at _" "Made exclusively for

_" "Many are called but few are chosen." And simply, "Hurry."

How to send the scarcity signal

It's easy! Make your proposition special, and limited. Limited time. Limited opportunity. Limited resources. Or make it special, and exclusive. We'll be the first ones to get it done. Or, offer a first peek at a growing trend. Or, identify a unique opportunity that will never come again. Or, only give out enough information to keep people's interest. Need I say more?

How to stop when the clock is ticking:

When someone tries to sway you with the scarcity signal, here is how to protect yourself from possible bad intent. It's easy. Just think for yourself! Just because something is limited doesn't mean it's better. Just because something is scarce doesn't mean it is in demand. And just because something is exclusive, doesn't mean it works any better than something else. Calm down and ask yourself, is this really something you need to have? What if it wasn't in demand? If there were no clock ticking down the remaining time, would you need it? Consider it on its own to determine the real value to you.

Try this while you can

Take a few minutes to consider how to add the signal of scarcity to your persuasion proposition. Then, if there are no questions or objections, I'll meet you in the next chapter on dealing with questions and objections!

25

QUESTIONS? OBJECTIONS?

To succeed at the art of persuasion, you must be open to, invite even, any questions on the mind of your persuadee. Left unanswered, those questions will work steadily in the background to undo your persuasion work, until your persuadee talks himself out of change and winds up exactly back where he began. Questions are an exciting indicator that a person is interested in your proposal. What an opportunity! Your goal, when asked a question, is to understand and then answer the question.

Always backtrack a question before answering it

To better understand a question, repeat it back using the exact words used to ask it. This increases affinity and acceptance through blending, and gives you a second chance to hear the question, to notice what information it provides, and what information is missing.

Notice the time element and accessing language

The question may have a time element (past, present or future) and an accessing element (sight sound or feeling.) Make certain that your response incorporates these elements, so that it is well targeted to the interests of your questioner.

You can reframe and answer your own question

If you have an answer, by all means give it. If you are not in a situation where you can ask questions of your questioner, you'll have to guess the deeper meaning, restate the question with this new meaning, and then respond to that. Then ask the questioner to affirm that you answered the question. "Does that answer that for you?"

Reflect the question back to the questioner

If someone is asking for your feelings, thoughts or views, you can always reflect that back to her by asking "How do you feel about it?" or "What are your thoughts?" or " How do you view this?"

If you don't know the answer, you can admit it

When you don't know the answer to a question, you have three options for answering the question.

- Say, "I don't know." and then ask if anyone else does
- Say "I don't know," and offer to find out.
- Reframe the question, and answer the new question. "I think the question you're asking me is _ and the answer is _."

If you feel cornered, get others involved.

If you ever feel cornered by the way a question is asked, that's a great time to ask others to get involved and broaden the discussion. "I'm interested in hearing what others think about this. Anyone? Tashina, how would you answer this question?"

If you feel undermined, be a pro, focus forward.

Be professional. Say you're sorry that they feel that way, but you appreciate their honesty. Use the relevancy question. "When you say _, what does that have to do with _?"

Deal with opposition.

In the next chapter, we'll explore how to deal with opposition. For now, a simple strategy is to interrupt a person who is attacking you in a tactful way, by repeating the person's name or gender over and over and over until he or she stops and asks, "What?" Then, say thank you for the question, offer to discuss it privately, and state or restate your intention to go forward. If you like, you can always let them have the last word, but you decide where and when. "At the end of the meeting, I'm willing to discuss this with you further." Or "When I've finished my presentation, I'm willing to answer any questions you might have."

Deal with objections.

Since the dawn of time, the best ideas have been met with doubts and fears. The year is somewhere between 5000 and 6000 years ago. Picture a cave in a forest. Two men, Ugh and Moogh, are having a discussion. Ugh recommends a circular shape for transportation. Moogh doubts that it will work. Ugh demonstrates a small model (a branch that he rolls down a hill.) Moogh thinks it was dumb luck. Ugh is tempted to think Moogh is dumb. But lucky Ugh, he interprets Moogh's doubts as interest, thanks him for speaking up, and proceeds to convert Moogh's objections into persuasion. And that, boys and girls, is why, to this very day, the wise persuader loves objections whenever they are raised.

Of course, it could happen that Ugh calls Moogh dumb, and Moogh then gathers an army by raising the call that some idiot named Ugh is trying to upset the applecart (which they don't even have yet,) and before you know it, Ugh is staring at the business end of several sharp sticks held by fierce opponents with blood in their eye! YIKES! What I'm saying here is that your well thought out presentation may, through something you say or do, don't say or don't do, either create opposition, or at least bring it to the surface in a most obvious way.

I used to believe that a lack of objections was a good sign. I've since learned that a lack of objections may be a signpost up ahead that you've entered the "Uncommitted" zone. It turns out that objections are a good thing. Why good? Because understood correctly, an objection is a request for more information. Your persuadee may not realize it, but the fact that he's given you an objection means he has an interest in learning more. And when someone raises an objection, there is a good chance that she represents others who share that objection but, due to shyness or some other fear, wouldn't speak up if their lives depended on it. Once an objection is voiced, you have the opportunity to address it and eliminate it.

The worst possible response to an objection is a defensive drive to stop it, dismiss it, or otherwise destroy without ever finding out what it is and what's behind it. So the best initial response to an objection is not "Ugh!" but "Thank you!" Thanks to an objection, you have a precious opportunity to be persuasive at a more meaningful and motivational level.

The basic rule: Don't lie or exaggerate

Lying and exaggeration on critical points or ideas are likely to undermine your credibility and damage your persuasion proposition. It's just not worth the risk. All it takes is to be exposed in a single falsehood, and no matter how true the rest of what you say, your entire proposition falls apart. While exaggeration is great in the funny business, answering objections isn't supposed to be funny. (Well, a little humor is a good thing, but seriously, serious questions deserve serious answers!) If the facts don't support you, admit it, and then give other facts. If there are disadvantages to your proposal, admit to them honestly and then emphasize the advantages. Since there's no such thing as a perfect decision, you want to help people make their best decision. You put your best foot forward by being straightforward.

Inoculation - Bring up the objection first!

If you can predict an objection, you can plan for it. Over the years, I have learned in my public speeches and seminars about the kinds of things I say that might be objectionable. I'd rather prevent predictable objections from being raised whenever possible, so as to make room for new objections. I do this by building in the objection and responding to it before anyone else has the chance to object. This has had the added benefit of helping me improve my presentations.

People may not always know why they object to something, but if you show an interest, you are likely to find out. Maybe they are worried about a possible conflict or complication. Maybe they want to be certain that you really know what you're talking about. Maybe it is an expression of self-doubt. In any case, and in every case, a systematic approach to dealing with objections is likely to give you the best possible result, whether it's a merge with someone else's proposition, or their adoption of yours. The gist of your objection system goes like this. First, thank the person who offered the objection. Second, find out what it is. Third, find out what's behind it. Fourth, provide information that speaks to the deeper interest.

Find out what's behind it

Handling objections is less about telling and selling an idea, and more about caring about the person and sharing your knowledge and or information. Once you've found out what you can about what's behind an objection, here's how to respond.

Money objections are about value

The objection is "This is too expensive." The art of persuasion is about speaking to the interests of others, not convincing them to do what is not in their own interest. But money objections are almost always about value. People who claim there's no money for something seem to find money for something else. If it costs more, then it should be worth more. That's why money objections are opportunities to build value.

You can build value by comparing costs. "Expensive compared to what?" Then compare the benefits of your proposition versus the one of lesser cost.

You can build value by breaking the cost down into an 'amount per day,' or 'amount per week,' or 'amount per item' and comparing that amount to something for which your persuadee already spends that kind of money

You can build value by adding up the benefits and asking how much they would be worth to your persuadee.

You can build value by reminding your persuadee of statements they've previously made regarding their interests and motivations.

If the objection made already includes a comparison to something less expensive, as in "I can get something that works just as well for half the price!" simply agree that she can get something at half the price, but with less than half the value of your proposition. Then highlight the benefits and advantages of your proposition as compared with the less expensive idea. Whatever you say, whatever you compare, you want to build value.

Feature comparisons are about benefits

The objection is that your product or service doesn't do what the current product or service does, or what a competing product or service does. "Yours doesn't have this particular feature." That's a signal to find out more about the feature to which he is referring. Remember, people care about features because of the benefits they provide, and make decisions based on benefits, not features.

You can find out whether or not the feature in the other product or service is essential. Ask how often it is used or what makes it important. The information revealed might tell you exactly what you need to know in order to answer the objection effectively. If a missing feature does something significant, acknowledge it. Then focus on a feature missing in the other product or service that is present in yours, and how that provides a greater benefit.

You can point to unique features in your own product or service that offer advantages to the features in older or

210

competing products and services, and translate those features into benefits.

Feeling objections are about fear and procrastination

The purpose of some objections is to delay progress. This is the best trick of procrastinators, who fear making the wrong choice and either getting blamed for it or feeling responsible for it. When ever you receive an objection that seems to serve only to delay making a decision, that's a signal not for more information, but for some handholding, patience and questions.

Zig Ziglar, the famous motivational speaker and sales trainer, taught that the best response to feeling statements was his Feel, Felt, Found formula. "I understand how you can feel that way. I've known others who felt that way. What they found was...' and then offer encouragement that your proposition meets their needs and interests. You can use natural language for this. In fact, the pattern works because this is a natural response when identifying with someone's objection and knowing how you found resolution for yourself. It becomes a personal testimonial. "I understand. I had the same issue. But then I realized..."

Deferring to a higher authority indicates doubt

The objection goes like this: "I have to talk to my husband/wife/employees/boss/partner first." This is an indicator of doubt, and a signal for reassurance. The best response is "That's a good idea. I always talk things over before making important decisions too." This helps your persuadee to feel safe and understood. Next, there are two things you can inquire about to great effect. First, you could simply ask, and "What part of my proposition will you discuss with _?" Explore this with your persuadee and she may reveal her doubts to you. You can then speak to those doubts, and ask for a decision. Or, you can ask if _____ is the decision maker. If the answer is yes, ask to speak to this person yourself. That may prompt your persuadee to make the decision herself, rather than leave you with the impression that she doesn't have the authority.

Time objections are about delay or detail

When the objection is 'I don't have time for this right now," your persuadee is either putting off having to hear your proposition until you give up and go away, or he realizes that there are details missing that require more time and attention. In either case, say that you understand, and appreciate that he recognizes the importance of giving your proposal the attention it deserves. Then ask, "When is a better time?" It is in your interest to keep some control by making the next contact instead of waiting for it.

If the objection is that your proposal would take too much time to implement, find out how much time is wasted under the current system. If the objection is that there isn't enough time to implement your proposal, that's a signal that more detail is needed about how it can work.

In each case, you have the opportunity to take a next step in handling the objection.

Now it's up to you

With that, we're out of time for more questions. If there are no objections, take the next few minutes and consider what questions and objections your persuasion proposition is likely to raise or provoke. Then apply what you've learned in this chapter to strengthening your proposition. Then I'll meet you in the next chapter, where we'll face and tackle outright opposition!

26

DEALING WITH OPPOSITION

"You'll never change my mind." "I wasn't born yesterday! Who do you think you're kidding?" "Save your breath. We've got better things to do than listen to another of your foolish ideas!"

The biggest mistake that you can make when faced with opposition is to turn the encounter into a confrontation. It's not hard to do. Talk down, put it down, or go round in an argument. "Yes, but..." will surely deepen it. "You're wrong!" forces others to choose sides. And what becomes of you and your ideas? You wind up weakened where you might have had support.

I speak from experience. I learned this the hard way, in the beginning of my professional speaking career. And I had an audience for the lesson. I'll never forget that queasy feeling as the group turned against me. I'll never forget my astonishment at how easily everything I said seemed to turn into something else.

213

DEALING WITH OPPOSITION

It was an evening seminar on lasting love in a fickle world. The audience was mostly single. There was a young man in the audience, sitting between two young women, and trying to impress both. He was talking each in turn, back and forth, and loud enough to disrupt and distract everyone else, and me in particular. Ever so politely, I asked him to please lower his voice for the benefit of the people around him, or take the conversation outside. He took that as a signal to get louder.

Then I asked him what his problem was. He replied, "What's your problem?" I defended my position. "I'm trying to do my job up here, and what you are doing isn't working for me or the people sitting around you." His reply, "Maybe I'm doing them a favor. Because you don't know what you're talking about anyway." It went straight downhill from there, as everything I said made it worse for me, and better for him. By evening's end I was exhausted, most of the group had left, except those who stayed to watch the conflict and see how it ended. The good news is that it did end. The bad news is that it ended badly. I asked him to leave. He wouldn't. I had the full experience of dealing with opposition, and I hated it.

The funny thing is, I had other choices that evening. I might have had an entirely different experience if I had gotten the group involved. I could have been curious as to why he was there and how it was working out for him. I could have pointed out that he seemed well on his way to finding lasting love, what with the two lovelies sitting beside him, and invited him to tell us all what he knew on the subject of healthy relationships. I could have called a break. I could have asked the facility manager to send security. Any of these options would have been better than turning his behavior into a confrontation.

I don't know if this guy had a legitimate grievance, just wanted some attention, or was trying to impress the two women. I suspect the latter, but what difference does it make? If he had a legitimate problem, he had plenty of opportunities to express his position, but he never did. Sometimes difficult people are not opposed to you or your idea – they're just intentionally annoying to draw attention. Difficult people are a test of your flexibility and self-control. Persuasive people refuse to be distracted by annoying others. Persuasive people manage these relationships.

If something like what happened to me ever happens to you while presenting your ideas to a group, maintain your professionalism and choose one of the following options instead.

It's not personal

Let's face it. Life is hard and some people do not know how to ask for help. Some don't know how receive it when offered. All that is left to them is to share their difficulty and discouragement by dumping it on others. But it isn't personal, ever, and as you build your character and inner strength and resolve, you discover that these people have no control over you.

I recall a person who I worked for years ago who was so incredibly negative and angry, who said the meanest, most accusatory things imaginable. I decided to treat this negativity as a hot wind, and to weather it. I made a game of it, quietly telling myself the opposite of whatever awful thing he said about me. After awhile, I looked forward to that blast of wind, because of how much it got me to affirm myself, my life, and my efforts to influence things for the better. He would walk away angry, and I would walk away elated.

You can take a break

Like the song says, you've got to know when to hold 'em, and know when to fold 'em. Sometimes, you call time out, recoup your losses, regroup and regain control. Some conversations are better as a private interaction than a spectator sport.

Include others in the discussion

If you are unable to bring a determined opponent around to your side, then go around them by bringing others in who may have influence in the situation.

"Maybe I'm the only one here who finds this distracting. How about the rest of you?" Then be quiet and wait. Or go around the room. Someone will respond. And chances are, they will express agreement with you about the difficult behavior. "Apparently, I'm not the only one here having a problem with this. Let's talk about this after the program. Moving on." Remember, you don't need the buy in of every person in order to move forward.

Try the tactful interruption

There are two ways to use the tactful interruption. Repeat his name or gender over and over and over again until you have his attention. Say "Sir. Sir. Sir," until he says "What?" Then, firmly but not aggressively, offer to let him have the last word, only at the time and place of your choosing. You say "Thank you for your feedback. You can either stay and talk with me on the break, or, if you find no value in being here, you are welcome to leave, and we'll happily refund your money. It's your choice. I want to do the right thing for everyone here. Moving on.

In some situations, your opposition is driven by deep-seated emotions that have nothing to do with you. When that's the case, chances are that you are not alone in dealing with it, as he makes trouble for everyone else too. Maybe he needs medication, maybe he needs therapy, or maybe he needs medication and therapy. Since his behavior is about his needs rather than your proposition, your actions should be designed to minimize his disruptive behavior. You can use the tactful interruption, "Joe, Joe, Joe," until he says, "What?" and then pick right back up where you left off as if the interruption never occurred.

Get Curious

Sometimes opposition represents a position deserving of your curiosity and even respect. Just because a person has little in the way of persuasion skills does not disqualify them from having a valid position. Since all behavior has a purpose, ask yourself, "What does this person really want?" Or, ask them. "When you say (backtrack what they've just said,) "What are you really trying to say? What is it that you want right now?" With this information, you either bring them around, or work around them.

Sow Seeds of Doubt

If the person you seek to persuade has a strong position, you might find it easier to respond if you first sow a few seeds of doubt using the information gate questions, like "How do you know?" and "According to whom?" and "What would happen if you did?" Remember though, with strong positions, you only want to question a part of it while protecting the rest of it.

Play the polarity

You can prescribe a contrarian's position, and force him to abandon it. I call this playing the Polarity Response. The Polarity Response is a built in mechanism inside all of us that hates being told what to think and what to do. Another way to think of the polarity response is that it is the teenage part of you that has yet to grow up. Playing off this response requires you to agree with the person opposing you, and then take a position more extreme than theirs. She says, "It won't work." And you agree. "You're right. It won't work. Not even you could find a way to make it work." If the person opposing you is a contrarian, then the only way she can remain opposed to you is to flip to your position! "Oh yeah? It will work, and here's how!"

You tell him, "Ok, you're right. I don't know what I'm talking about. There's no way someone like you could ever, ever get anything of any value from a program like this. Not a chance." He can protest. "I could if I wanted to." Now you disagree with him. "No, I don't think so. Not even you could learn something in this seminar." He's trapped on the horns of a dilemma. He can be quiet. He can leave. I n any case, you met him where he was, and he had to deal with you. But don't be surprised if he flips. "Go ahead, let's see what you've got." To which you can reply, "Thank you. Moving on."

Command respect

Another option with opponents is to earn their respect. This is absolutely essential when dealing with people who are hostile and aggressive. You do this by conducting yourself in such a way that they can't help but admire your self-possession and self-control in dealing with them. Take charge over your breathing first. Slow it down and drop it into your diaphragm area. Then plant your feet firmly on the ground and grow some roots. Think before you talk. Be direct and to the point.

Make the covert overt

Some opposition might be driven by the desire to punish you or get even with you. You know the saying, 'When might won't make right, revenge is a dish best served cold.' When someone is out to get you, they may attack you openly or covertly, to your face or behind your back. If the attack is covert instead of overt, based in sarcasm rather than information, odds are that you are dealing with someone who feels out of control, and who believes their best chance at having some control is to undermine your self-control. To bring hidden agendas and grudges to the surface directly, repeat back a sarcastic remark and then ask for its relevance to your proposal. "I'm talking about (this). What does (that) have to do with (this?)"? Or you can repeat it back and then ask for the intention behind it. "When you say that, what are you really trying to say?"

If he denies any intent at all, let it go. Keep up this pattern and the covert opponent learns that you're going to call him on his bad behavior every time he engages in it. If, instead, he eventually decides to tell you what's really going on, listen, and help him to express his grievance, frustration or problem with you fully. When he's done, thank him for his honesty, and let him know that in the future he can deal with you in a more direct and professional manner.

Don't be a wimp

Opposition, schmopposition. Right now, take a stand with your proposition and scan the horizon. Are there any who dare oppose you? If so, how can you use the material in this chapter to increase your persuasive power? Confidence comes from preparation. If opposition is predictable, then go ahead and predict it and plan for it.

Meanwhile, how do you keep an entire group from turning on you? I'll be waiting in the next chapter to tell you all about it.

27

RICK'S RULES FOR MEETINGS

The worst case scenario for group discussion is when everyone is against you and you're fairly certain that you're on your own. If you ever find yourself trapped in that tiny space between a rock and a hard place, then stop and regroup. Back up, back off, buy some time and step back into the fray when you have a plan and a purpose. Use the interim time to find your allies, because there is strength in numbers. If you can't find anyone to support you, that is likely feedback that you're on the wrong track. Lick your wounds, learn from the experience, and move on, all the wiser for it.

The best-case scenario for group discussions is that they are focused, not on personalities and bad behavior, but on ideas to be considered and outcomes to be achieved. But groups consist of individuals, and individuals do sometimes have competing interests, hidden agendas, and difficult behavior. The result is that it is all too common for group time to become wasted time, where arguments and angry conflict poisons the atmosphere and interferes with any possibility of progress.

The way to make the best use of meetings and avoid the worst of people is with ground rules established at the outset, and leadership that holds the group accountable for those rules. Once these ground rules exist, it is essential that they are posted someplace visible in the meeting room, and reviewed at the outset of a meeting. Then get consent from each person in attendance to abide by the rules.

Hold the focus.

Your group should decide at the beginning of the meeting what it wants to accomplish, why it wants to accomplish it, and why getting that result matters. This makes it easier, when meetings skid off track, to use the relevancy question to bring it back.

Here's the rule: Begin meetings with the end in mind. First establish what we're doing and why we're doing it and why it matters.

Later, if the meeting starts to go off track, it's easy for someone (you) to say, "We said the reason for this meeting is such and such. What does what we're talking about have to do with such and such?"

Listen when others talk

Meetings lose momentum when people quit listening to each other, or listen only for what they disagree with, or start making things up about what they hear.

Here's the rule: Listen to each other the way you want others to listen to you. You are accountable for understanding each other, and you ask questions to clarify what you don't understand.

Later, if the meeting starts to off on a tangent because of a misunderstanding, you can invoke the rule. "We said we would ask questions to clarify what we don't understand. Dave, what is the question you need to ask right now?"

Everyone gets a chance to talk.

Some of us like to talk. Some of us do not. Some of us are quick to offer ideas, and some of us need time to think.

Here's the rule: Limit the amount of time for any individual to speak in order to give everyone a chance to speak on each topic.

Later, if someone is doing all the talking, someone (you) can invoke the rule. "We agreed to limit the amount of time for any individual to speak in order to give everyone a chance to speak. Let's go around the table and hear what others have to say."

Find common ground.

When we attend meetings, we actually have more in common than we may realize. It's important to get to common ground when there is any potential for conflict.

Here's the rule: Whenever disagreement is a possibility, identify what you can agree on first.

Later, if a discussion begins to devolve into conflict, someone (you) can invoke the rule. "We agreed that whenever disagreement is a possibility, we would identify what we can agree on first. What are the areas of this discussion where we agree?"

Consider Multiple Views

The more (points of view) the merrier! The grand mystery of great meetings is synergy, where all of us are smarter than any of us. Each of us has a unique way of paying attention, and each of us has the potential of seeing what is in everyone else's blind spot. Great meetings take this into account

Here's the rule: All of you are smarter than any of you (SYNERGY). Consider all points of view offered in the meeting to be as valid as your own, and consider each point of view before settling on any one view in particular.

Later, if someone gets locked into a position, some-one (you) can invoke the rule. "We each agreed to consider all points of view as valid to our own, and to consider each point of view before settling on one. I'd like to review all of our options."

Discuss differences respectfully.

The problem with publicly voiced insults and hostile remarks is that bad blood stains the carpet, the drapes, and the furniture. Once bad blood is spilled through verbal mis-behavior, the consequence is that it occupies the shared feeling space. Better to prevent, or at the least, redirect this energy before someone gets (their feelings) hurt.

Here's the rule: No hostile or insulting remarks. Talk to each other the way you want others to talk to you. Treat them with the same level of respect that you desire for your-self.

Later, if someone gets plugged in and starts acting out, someone (you) can invoke the rule: "We agreed not to use hostile or insulting remarks. Let's take a moment, calm down, and approach this again in a reasonable manner."

Find the good

No matter how bad a problem is, every silver lining has a dark cloud. No wait, every dark cloud has a silver lining! But it may be hidden from view. That's why it is important to find the good, even in the difficult.

Here's the rule: When you are critical of an idea, consider the benefits of the idea as part of your evaluation of it.

Later, if people become too critical to make progress, someone (you) can invoke the rule. "We agreed to consider benefits of ideas along with criticism. I think it's time to revisit that."

Solutions are better than blame

I've heard it said that whatever you focus on expands. I don't know if that's exactly true, but I do know that groups that succeed in assigning blame aren't particularly effective in changing anything for the better. Groups that focus on finding solutions generally do, and the side effect is a dynamic and creative environment that brings out the best in people. Solutions are more valuable than blame.

Here's the rule: Learn from the past, and then apply what you've learned to the future.

Later, if the meeting devolves into finger pointing, someone (you) can invoke the rule. "We agreed to learn from the past and apply what we've learned to the future.

What can we learn from this mistake that is valuable for the future?"

Have a meeting with yourself

That ends our exploration of objections and opposition. I hope you didn't find it too objectionable. Please apply this to your persuasion proposition, and do your best to anticipate objections and opposition, and plan your responses. Then, to bring our exploration of talking to a close, turn to the next chapter to learn about closing!

28

CLOSING

There are two aspects of closing a persuasive proposition that I now want to bring to your attention. The first is about 'sealing the deal,' and the second is about how you feel. In this chapter we'll deal with the former. In the next chapter, the latter.

In sales parlance, a 'close' is when you complete the persuasion process and bring your persuadee to a moment of decision. Some sales people believe that everything you say from the moment you first engage a person to the moment you finish is directed at that moment of decision. And indeed, if you did a great job of listening and understanding the needs, intentions, motivations and positions of your persuadee, and you've targeted this information in the way you presented yours, closing ought really to be a matter of asking for the decision. If only it were so simple.

Because of the desire to conserve mental energy whenever possible, the most common and easily made deci-

226

sion a person can make is 'I'll deal with this later.' And the most likely response to your request for a decision is the fear of making the wrong choice. You do both yourself and your persuadee a favor by bringing the proposition to a close and getting a definitive decision. A successful closing means one less thing for both of you, or all of you, to carry over into the future.

Closing carries a sense of finality with it. Closed. Over. Done. So it may be helpful to work your way to it with a series of smaller decisions, rather than jumping to the end. We've discussed at length the value of open-ended questions in the listening phase of persuasion. At the closing end of your proposition, you use closed-ended questions instead. Close-ended questions require either a yes or a no. They being with 'Did I?' 'Did you?' 'Am I?' 'Are you?' 'Do I?' 'Do you?' 'Will I?' 'Will you?' 'Have I?' 'Have you?' There's not a what, who, where, when or how to be found.

And in the case of a successful close, you want to ask questions that invite a yes response. That means you have to know the answer is yes before you ask the question.

When asking for a yes, nod your head up and down to signify that a yes answer is the correct one. Verbally and non-verbally, this collection of behavior is called 'Building a Yes Set.' A yes set creates momentum for a positive response to your final question, the one in which you ask for the decision. 'Can I place your order?' or 'Do I have a green light to proceed?' Of course, once the decision is made, you can go back to open ended questions to get the details of what happens next, when it happens, where it happens, and how it happens.

Building a Yes-Set

I've been told of an urban legend regarding the Yes-Set Close. It goes like this: If you can get a person to say yes eight times in a row, you will close a sale. I've not been able to track down any studies that prove it, but it serves well as a useful assumption.

Here is an example of a series of questions designed to get a YES response.

Do you feel that I have understood your needs and interests?

Did I address all of your concerns regarding this?

Do you have enough information to understand what this is?

Do you have enough information to understand how it works?

Do you understand how you will benefit from this?

Wouldn't you love to be receiving all these benefits right now?

Do you understand how this is able to produce these benefits?

If it works as I've said, is it a good choice for you?

What if you get a NO?

What if you get a no instead of a yes at any point in the close? Then you must stop and learn about what is in the way before beginning to close again. And if all you get are no's, well, you can't win them all. As a persuasive friend of mine says it, "Some will, some won't. So what. Some are waiting." Don't keep wasting time on a losing proposition. Wrap it up as gracefully as you can, and move on. There is really only so much that you can do. This part of it is now out of your hands.

What if you get a MAYBE?

If you keep getting a maybe instead of a clear yes or a clear no, that is a clear indication that you haven't listened well enough. Stop pressing forward and drop your agenda. Pay attention, ask questions and find the MAP before returning to your persuasion proposition.

The final question

Assuming, however, that you've gotten your yes responses, now it's time for your final question. It's a good idea to figure this out and practice it a few times, so you can do it naturally and authentically when closing your persuasion proposition.

Your final question begins with a summary of benefits, and other important information about prices, discounts, and timing. Then you ask for the sale, for the agreement, or for the green light to proceed. This is where your internal state has a lot to do with your external result. If your insides are saying yes with confidence, you are likely to get a yes in response. If, on the other hand, you are doubtful or afraid of rejection, guess what is likely to happen? Yep. They'll say nope. And if your persuadee feels too much pressure in your question, or detects that you are attached to the outcome, these factors are off putting and will get in your way.

Instead, detach from the result. Let go. You've given it your best, and it is now out of your control and in the control of your persuadee. But you still have a choice. You can ask for the decision, "May I place your order," or act as if you have it and end with an offer to act on the decision. "If you'll give me your credit card number, I'll place your first order for you." Whichever you choose, be as natural and gentle as possible. Then smile, wait, and enjoy the fact that whatever happens, you've learned a lot and done your best to be of service to your persuadee's needs, interests and motivations with your persuasion proposition.

Put the logic in writing

Once you've got a favorable decision to support your proposition, you have a little tidying up to do in order to keep the decision alive after you walk away.

Leave the logical part of the agreement in writing. This gives your persuadee something to look at to remind them of the evidence that justified the decision they just made. Remember, most decisions are made emotionally, and then logic is used to justify the decision after it's been made.

Make yourself available to answer questions after the fact, as an added value to the agreement or decision.

Offer other assurances and reminders about the benefits their decision will provide, and how delighted you are to have their agreement.

Time for you to close on your proposition

Stop. Read no further, until you take some time to apply the material in this chapter to your persuasion proposition. Don't worry; I'm not going anywhere. I'll be right here as soon as you've done that. Allow me to repeat. Stop. Read no further until after you take the time to apply the material in this chapter to your persuasion proposition.

Now it's time to change the subject one last time. And this time, right here and right now, we will be exploring the most powerful characteristic of persuasive people, organized around a single idea. I call it Presence. Turn to the next chapter and Be There Now! (Be here then?)

29

PRESENCE

I admit it. I love speaking to groups. Whether it's
five people or 5000 people, I find the relationship and interaction with people in my audience to be incredibly
stimulating and fulfilling. Yet speaking in public is often
cited as the number one fear of adults. The Book of Lists
places the fear of death in fifth place while public speaking
ranks first. Comedian Jerry Seinfeld interprets this to mean
that, at a funeral, people would much rather be in the casket
than giving the eulogy. That's astonishing! How can that
possibly be?

There are at least a couple of ways to explain this
anxiety, one physical, and the other psychological. The psychological aspect of presenting ideas has to do with self
doubt and the fear of being found out, with negative self talk,
with poor role models and the subsequent mental scripts and
images people follow when called upon to 'represent' an
idea, a plan, a choice, a product or service. The physical side
of this anxiety is a result of the psychological aspect, and it's

the part of presentation that is most problematic for you, the persuader. Shaky voice. Flushed skin. Sick to the stomach. Feel ill. Nausea rising. Armpits sweating. Losing train of thought. Whoa, who wants to go through that?

First, for the fun of it, how about some wild speculation on how the psychological fear of public presentation develops! Maybe there were moments of public humiliation in our past that gave birth to the fear? (If that's you, you know what I'm talking about!) Maybe you expect too much, but prepare too little. Maybe it's from watching too much television, because everyone on TV knows just what to say, and laugh tracks make it seem so normal for people to be entertaining when talking. Or maybe it's the kind of things you say to yourself, words of discouragement and doubt, projected on your mental screen as a worst-case scenario. Or maybe the idea of presentation gets frozen from a verb into a noun, a freezer, which leads to dissociation from your internal resources. And maybe, just maybe, it is the result of a false idea about how obvious your anxiety must be to others. Why false? Because nervousness always, yes, always, feels more intense than it looks!

The good news is that you don't have to overcome anxiety and nervousness. You just have to control it, learn to work with it, use the energy created by it to your advantage. Here are a few controls that can help you increase your persuasive presence.

Breathe low and slow

When you experience fear, anxiety and nervousness, your body undergoes changes. And one of the first changes is in your breathing. There are three basic ways you can breathe. High and shallow, middle and regular, low and slow. High and shallow is the breathing of stress. Middle and regular is automatic breathing, the kind that happens when you are going about your daily business. Low and slow breathing is the breathing of intentional relaxation. Guess which kind of breathing gives you the greatest benefit when you are giving a presentation? Yes, it's low and slow. This kind of breathing involves your diaphragm, and when you do it your stomach protrudes on the inhale. Low breathing grounds you and connects you to yourself. Fear drives breathing higher up in the chest, leading to gasping, sputtering, and oxygen deprivation! This high and fast breathing puts pressure on your voice box, and reverberates through your body, out to your hands (shaking) and knees (shaky) and stomach (upset) and voice (strained.)

Known in the breathing biz as diaphragmatic breathing, low and slow allows you to maximize the amount of oxygen getting in to your system. I suggest you practice this until you are good at it, because new habits involve repetition and intensity. Try it now! Place a couple of fingers on your diaphragm (about halfway between your nipples and your belly button!) Then breathe in, and if you've involved your diaphragm correctly, it will push your fingers away from your body. Do this really slowly, counting up to 10 or even 20. Then let go. Do this before beginning a presentation, and you will find that as you gain some breathing control, you get some control over your hands, your feet, and your voice at the same time.

Press your fingers and toes

Here's another relaxation method you can use while you are presenting! Just press your first finger and thumb together as hard as you can. This creates a pressure point that draws your unconscious attention away from nervousness and into the point. Or, if you prefer, squish your toes into the floor as hard as you can. When you stop pressing your toes, your body will relax a little. Do it again, your body will relax a little more. Or do them both together. Between diaphragmatic breathing and finger and toe pressing, you can calm yourself and increase your persuasive presence.

Use a symbolic gesture

No, not that one! Instead, you can create a symbolic and empowering anchor/gesture and use it any time you are about to speak in a persuasive manner. Johnny Carson, before walking out on stage, swung an invisible golf club. One of my clients is in public office, and he pumps his fist in the air before speaking. These gestures, once built and rehearsed, provide the strength and confidence needed to speak clearly and persuasively. I built one year ago. Now, when I walk out in front of any group, I hold my hands apart with palms up, and then bring them together with a clap, clasping them in front of me.

The basic idea is pick a gesture, identify what it means to you, build it, practice it, and use it. Here's how to build one for yourself. First, decide what it will be. It could be a hand movement or an arm movement or a leg movement, or interacting with an invisible prop. Next, plant your feet firmly on the ground. Bend your knees a little. Next, put your conscious attention into the area around your belly button. Relax your shoulders. Then, remember a time when you were excited, happy, confident and eager, and had all the time in the world. This remembered experience does not have to have anything to do with speaking. It could be at a ballgame or a concert, sitting with your sweetheart alongside a stream, any experience where you have the physical sensations and or emotions that you desire to have in speaking. As you remember those positive feelings, make your symbolic gesture. Rinse. Repeat!

Repeat this process several times, and you will train your nervous system to give you those sensations when you make that gesture. It's called stimulus-response, and you can strengthen it through intensity and repetition. You can even practice it in the imaginary future! Imagine yourself doing this pattern just before your presentation, and having the experience of calm, confidence and persuasive power that you desire. Enjoy it. Yes!

Talk to yourself

I once heard anxiety described as 'letting your inner child operate the adrenalin controls of your body.' I believe this is a reference to the out of date and mistaken notions people often develop about themselves as children, and that are reinforced in adulthood as negative self-talk in moments of fear or vulnerability. Instead of listening reactively to your own negative self-talk like "I can't handle this," or " I'm the wrong person in the wrong place at the wrong time," you want to learn and practice speaking proactively to yourself about the pleasure you experience and the strength you have when speaking. Encouraging words do change physiological responses. Maybe not immediately, but with a little practice, they can and do.

Whenever you feel anxiety, there's no need to fight it. Accept it, and let yourself work with it rather than against it, to calm yourself down and regain your ability to focus and communicate.

One essential belief

I'm now about to share with you the one belief you need in order to succeed at the art of persuasion. It consists of four words. I will reveal these four words to you, and when I do, I want you to say them out loud, as if you believe then completely! Ready? Here they are:

YOU CAN DO IT!

PRESENCE

You have to believe that it's possible for you to successfully persuade your intended receiver. You have to believe in yourself. It only makes sense. If you're not persuaded that you can be persuasive, if you can't convince yourself that you can convince others, then there is no doubt that your persuasion efforts will be doubt-filled and, therefore, doubtful.

Remember the nature of sanity? Your results reflect your own attitudes in life and about persuasion. If you have a bad attitude about something, you can only persuade people who share your attitude. If you have a great attitude about something, you're more likely to persuade people to let you share it with them.

Some years ago, I was persuaded to watch a terrible movie by someone who persuaded me that it was delightful. There's no accounting for taste, and my tastes in movies were clearly different than my friend's. I found the characters exceedingly shallow (and this from a person like myself who enjoys cheesy movies!) and the plot almost non-existent. However, there was a memorable character in this movie. He was a gardener. And at the end of the film, when the hero drove away with his new bride, the gardener shouted after them: "You can do it!"

I can only guess as to what he was referring with these words. But the way he said it was infectious. The words and tone and accent stayed in my mind for months, and became a valuable resource when I was working on a book about dealing with relatives, an incredibly complex subject. Family means so many things to so many people in this day and age, and I wanted to create something powerful and effective to help people have positive family experiences. So I did hundreds of interviews, collected more data than I knew what to do with, and then tried dozens of ways to collate it and organize it to make it useful. There were times when I despaired of ever finishing the project.

And there came a moment when I had to persuade myself that if I couldn't complete the project, I would have to abandon it. That's when a funny thing happened. That voice spoke to me, in the privacy of my own mind. "You can do it!" I laughed. The voice continued, "You can! You can do it!" And all of a sudden, I changed my mind and the organizational scheme for the book on relatives presented itself clearly to my mind. Now I write all my books that way. Why? When it comes to persuasion propositions, I can do it! I can! And so can you!

There you have it, four simple methods to increase your persuasive presence. Breathing low and slow, pressing fingers and toes, using a symbolic gesture and talking positively to yourself about the one essential belief for you to be persuasive. We're ready to put a wrap on this book, so meet me in the next chapter where we'll draw our conclusions and then draw the curtains closed.

30

AND IN CONCLUSION

When people hear you talk, they tend to remember best what you started with and how you finished.

A great proposition always ends with a solid conclusion, rather than a forgettable end. And a great conclusion tends to follow the idea of "I told you what I'd tell you, and then I told you. Now let me tell you what I told you." A review of the main points of your persuasion proposition is essential, followed by either a review of actions taken or a call to action. This moment gives you another chance to help your persuadees revisit the ideas and information you've shared together, and it creates a runway for a perfect landing when you reach the end of your interaction.

In this book, I've offered you a view into the hidden secrets of the art of persuasion, and revealed how they work, why they work, and what to do when you want them to work for you. I defined three phases of a persuader's interaction with a persuadee, Listening, Transition, and Talking. We explored the nine information gates for understanding positions and helping people to change them. You learned about the eight persuasion guides and eight persuasion themes for packaging your information to make it easy to assimilate and appreciate. You learned seven persuasion signals for speaking to the emotions of your persuadee. We explored the Kirschner Model of Motivation, with six towards and away motivations for change. You learned about the 5 stages of change and the need to go one stage at a time in your persuasion efforts. You learned of the four possible persuasion outcomes, along with four communication need-styles of communication that can guide you in how to talk. You discovered that there are three receiving zones for new information, and that blending and other trust building activities are the fastest and best way into the acceptance zone. You recognized that people do indeed listen two very different ways, logically and emotionally, and you learned how to appeal to each. And you learned the one basic belief necessary for you to change your world with the art of persuasion.

Years ago, one of my persuasion mentors told me the secret to a great presentation is to "leave them laughing or leave them crying." It's great advice. It speaks yet again to the emotional nature of persuasive communication. And both laughter and tears humanize you, thus making your appeal more appealing. I've done both, and find both to be effective. I sometimes end my Art of Living programs with a story about a difficult time I went through when my daughter was small and I was struggling to earn enough income to support my family. It's a real story and very personal. It moves me every time I recall it and tell it. And it never fails to move my audience.

The secret to the power of that story is that when I share it, I am sharing an authentic moment in the story of my growth as a human being. You've had plenty such moments yourself. There is something profoundly liberating about drawing on your experience to share an experience with others. I encourage you to take some time and consider how you can leave your persuadees laughing or crying. In the art of persuasion, emotion makes the sale, and emotion closes it as well.

Just one more one more thing (yes, you read that correctly)

I want to share with you an experience I had many years ago. My wife and daughter accompanied me to a meeting of the International Platform Association in Washington D.C. The conference was fabulous. Ross Perot was a dinner speaker, and Colin Powell a speaker after lunch. There was a guy who looked and sounded like Teddy Roosevelt who spoke to us, and another who looked and sounded like Ben Franklin. We heard a diverse group of presenters on a wide array of topics, and a good time was had by all. On the last day, there was a contest for those in attendance who wanted to participate. The contest was a competition. In each round, you would give a one-minute speech in front of the whole conference audience. They would then, through a process of elimination, select a winner.

I thought it would be a lot of fun to do this with my daughter. She was a teenager at the time, she was on her high school debate team, and she had long had an interest in her dad's career. And I thought it would be fun to compete with her too, because even though she wasn't nearly as good as me, I thought she was pretty good and that it would be a real boost to her self esteem to compete against a pro!

So we signed up for the contest, and were divided into groups. One group at a time was taken to another room and instructed on how to speak and on what we would be judged. They told us what to do with our hands. They told us how to stand. They talked about what words to emphasize and how to emphasize them. They gave us a lot of input about speaking, and then sent us on stage, one at a time.

I had already been speaking professionally for a number of years at that point. I had my own style. I had my own way with words. I had confidence and strong material. But when they told us what the judges were looking for, I set aside everything I knew about speaking, and tried to do it their way. The result? I was eliminated in the first round! My daughter kept right on going. She beat me. Don't pity me. I'm okay with it. Mostly. But I learned a valuable lesson that day, and I want you to gain the benefit of my experience. Here's what I learned.

The most powerful persuasion comes from people who are natural and authentic. If you know something about persuasion that works for you, and I failed to mention it in this book, hey, do what you know to do, and let the information I've shared with you support you rather than hinder you. And if something I said in this book just does not work for you, please, don't do it! Fair enough?

I began this book talking about my desire to give people the tools to get their ideas across and change the world for the better. Now it's time for you to act on what you've read, and then act again, until the skills and strategies I've revealed to you become a natural part of the way you express yourself.

If I can leave you with one thing to take with you, to empower your creativity and enhance your persuasion skills, it is found in these words. YOU CAN DO IT! So go on! You're now an insider to the art of persuasion. So do it! Use your influence. Be persuasive. Change your mind, change your life, and change your world.

BIBLIOGRAPHY

Cialdini, Robert B. The Psychology of Influence.
New York: William Morrow & Co, 1993

Mills, Harry. Artful Persuasion, New York: AMACOM, 2000

Sprague, Jo and Stuart, Douglas. The Speaker's Handbook, Ft. Worth, TX: Hartcourt Brace & Company, 2000

Butterfield, Steve Booth. Steve's Primer of Practical Influence.
Online. 3 March 2005.
<http://www.healthyinfluence.com/Primer/primer.ht m>

Techniques for Changing Minds. Online. 10 July 2006.
<http://www.changingminds.org/techniques/techniqu es.htm>

Vorhaus, John. The Comic Toolbox. Los Angeles: Silman-James Press, 1994

Weissman, Jerry. Presenting to Win. New Jersey: FTPrentice Hall, 2003

ABOUT THE AUTHOR

Rick Kirschner is a respected faculty member of the Institute for Management Studies and an adjunct professor at Southwest College of Naturopathic Medicine (SCNM.edu). An Oregon-licensed naturopathic physician since 1981, Dr. Kirschner was in private practice from 1981-1987, and specialized in the treatment of stress disorders. From 1987-1992, he was one of only 15 presenters chosen by the Tom Peters Group to present the revolutionary 'In Search of Excellence' and 'Thriving On Chaos' training programs to businesses around the world.

Dr. Kirschner speaks to some of the world's best-known organizations, from Heineken to NASA to the Starbucks Coffee Company. He's fun, people relate to him, and he offers a palette of attitudes and behaviors that change lives, relationships and businesses for the better.

He is author or coauthor of 9 audio and video programs, including the bestselling "Dealing With Difficult People.' He is the coauthor of the international bestseller, "Dealing With People You Can't Stand: How To Bring Out The Best in People At Their Worst' (Brinkman and Kirschner, McGraw Hill.) Other books include Life By Design, Love Thy Customer, and Dealing With Relatives (e-book, available at TheArtofChange.com webstore)

He's been interviewed on hundreds of radio and television programs, including CNBC, FOX and CBC. His ideas on communication and conflict resolution are found in numerous newspapers and magazines including USA Today, London Times, The Wall Street Journal and Executive Excellence.

Dr. Kirschner resides in Southern Oregon with his wife and cats.

ALSO AVAILABLE FROM THE ART OF CHANGE LLC

SPEECHES and TRAINING

In keynote speeches for association events, in seminars and training for Fortune 1000 companies, and for executive and management retreats; in venues ranging from conference halls to grand theaters to meeting rooms, Dr. Rick Kirschner offers a powerful approach to dealing with change that unlocks creativity, enhances communication and increases commitment. He is persuasive, purposeful, and his programs consistently bring out the best in people. Dr. Kirschner can customize a presentation that supports the theme and objectives of your event. Bring The Art of Change Skills for Life™ to your organization!

COACHING and COUNSELING

Dr. Kirschner is a ready partner for change in the midst of your busy life. Are you ready for a change in your life? Then let Dr. Rick Kirschner help you to master The Art of Change! Benefits include increased clarity and confidence, better communication, stronger motivation, and lowered stress. Use the contact form at www.TheArtofChange.com.

The Art of Change LLC
P.O. Box 896, Ashland, OR 97520
541.488.2992 | drkinfo@theartofchange.com

ENEWS

Had enough of broken promises? Had it with people who just don't get you? Frustrated with pompous fools who don't have a clue? Don't get mad. Get help! The Art of Change ENEWS will give you insights into the why, how, and what you can do to change your life, your relationships, your work, and your world for the better! And it's absolutely free! You'll also get exclusive offers on books, audio and video programs by Dr. Kirschner. To subscribe, visit TheArtofChange.com

Audio programs
Dealing With Difficult People
    1 hour CD of Rick's live presentation

Insider's Guide To The Art of Persuasion
    8 CD comprehensive audio program

Living Your Life By Design
    1 hour CD of Rick's live presentation

Books
Dealing with People You Can't Stand
        (Brinkman and Kirschner, McGraw Hill, 2004)
        Bring out the best in people at their worst

Dealing With Relatives
        (Brinkman and Kirschner, e-Book)
        Your guide to successful family relationships

Life By Design
        (Kirschner and Brinkman, McGraw Hill 2002)
        A plan to bring out the best in yourself

Love Thy Customer
        (Brinkman and Kirschner, McGraw Hill 2006)
        Creating delight, preventing dissatisfaction

24 Lessons: Dealing With Difficult People
        (Brinkman and Kirschner, McGraw Hill 2006)

The Art of Change LLC, offering skills for life in keynote
speeches, teleconferences, private coaching, organizational
training, and information products for positive change.
You're invited to visit www.TheArtofChange.com.
Read the blog, listen to the podcast, and subscribe
to The Art of Change ENEWS.

Printed in the United States
119528LV00005B/313-318/A